To Bill,

I hope in some way this book helps you, your loved ones, and your clients.

all my best, your friend,

Vincent

WHAT OTHERS ARE SAYING ABOUT VINCENT LIBERTI AND THIS BOOK

"Vincent is like a trust whisperer. He has a way of being that needs to be learned by others, making this book a must read! When entering my Medicare years, finally I was determined to handle issues that seemed insurmountable to me, but which Vincent solved adeptly. He always was reachable, never made me feel incapable, and with his advice, gave me the ability to help myself. He didn't just do it for me; he educated me and had me involved every step of the way such that I felt more empowered with my own life. He helped me get the clarity I needed to create a better direction. This book also educates, empowers, and clarifies elder issues for the reader to solve for himself or herself."

— Nancy Moon, Entrepreneur

"*Preparing for Your Elder Years* is a valuable read for anyone who wants to get their ducks in a row for life. Vincent really knows his stuff."

— Jacqueline Voss Lees, J.D., LL.M., Connecticut and Massachusetts Estate and Elder Law Attorney

"Anyone who might soon care for an elderly loved one, or who themselves may be in their elder years, should consult Vincent's book. It is a wealth of information. I wholeheartedly recommend *Preparing for Your Elder Years* and his legal services. As a life care planner, I have worked with Vincent to help numerous clients with their estate planning, long-term care, and Medicaid concerns. It is a joy working with him and exchanging ideas on how to best help our clients. He is affable and excels at organizing and analyzing each client's unique situation to create a positive resolution. His book clearly presents many years of knowledge and experience as an estate and elder planning lawyer and law professor."

— Elena Goggin, Founder and Director of Elder Life Care Planning, LLC

"Vincent has a calm assuredness that overcomes the negative attorney stereotype, and I feel confident, comfortable, and well represented by him. Vincent has a knack for putting us at ease as he handles our legal situations, which he does with knowledge, skill, finesse, and competent legal prowess."

— Dr. Bayuk, Chiropractor and Musician

"This issue of end-of-life planning is vitally important. A member of my family owned a fiduciary company for more than forty years and helped many clients through these issues. Despite this, he did not have his affairs sufficiently in order before his own health suddenly deteriorated. He was unable to be consulted for information that only he knew, which caused a significant impact upon me, one of his clients, as well as other family members. Give yourself this gift—let Vincent guide you through these uncomfortable—yet necessary conversations. Only then can you have the peace of mind to focus on the things most important to you: whether it's connecting with Spirit, caring for your family, or fine-tuning your legacy that you'll leave for the world."

— J. Mathias Bennett, Leadership Advisor, Helping Entrepreneurs Lead with Confident Vulnerability

"After interviewing many estate planning lawyers, I chose Vincent as my lawyer for three main reasons: straightaway, I knew I could trust him; he answered the questions that *I* asked, and he didn't talk down to me as other estate planning lawyers tended to do. I made the right choice."

— Ms. P. Johnson, Happy Retiree

"Vincent combines his decades of legal experience in the areas of estate planning, elder law, and financial management with personal empathy and experience from providing for his own family. The result is a thoroughly readable, often poignant, and always enlightening look at a very hard topic. This will be the go-to guide for anyone looking for pragmatic advice and insight on planning for the senior years."

— Kelley G. Peck, J.D., LL.M., Connecticut Estate Planning Attorney, Author, Professor, Fellow of American College of Trust and Estate Council (ACTEC), Chair of Estate and Probate Connecticut Bar Association Committee

"I have been represented by Attorney Vincent Liberti for nearly five years, during which time he has successfully represented me in many legal matters. In each and every instance, I have been impressed by his responsiveness and professionalism in dealing with often complicated legal issues. Attorney Liberti is an able practitioner who skillfully and thoroughly conceptualizes potential issues and plans effective strategies that yield positive results. He has always gone the extra mile to completely familiarize himself with the pertinent aspects of my cases and thereby provided a comprehensive approach to my legal representation.

I enthusiastically recommend him as a competent and accomplished attorney who consistently delivers high quality services of tremendous value."

— Dr. R. M. Anastasio, Psychologist, Commercial Real Estate Investor

"As an established long-term care planner, I have been pleased to recommend several clients to Vincent for their estate planning and elder care needs. Besides his vast knowledge and integrity, Vincent's unique strength is the way he connects with people—he is extremely approachable and down to earth, and people feel at ease with him when discussing their important legal affairs. The feedback I have received from my clients has always been very positive. On a separate and more personal level, I really appreciate his desire to continually grow and learn so he can better serve his clients, and with *Preparing for Your Elder Years*, us all."

— Armen Abrahamian, CLTC, CSA, CIC
Long-Term Care Insurance Specialist

"As a young attorney, I was lucky enough to have Vincent as a law professor in estate planning and elder law. He has remained a mentor and colleague throughout the years. His extraordinary breadth of knowledge combined with a unique ability to make complex issues easily understandable for both students and clients is translated into the pages of *Preparing for Your Elder Years* in an easily accessible style. You can count on Vincent to present practical, useful material that has been honed to perfection during his years of practice and dedication to constant continuing education and teaching. He never rests on his laurels. Laypeople planning their finances at any stage of their lives, estate planning and elder law attorneys, as well as financial advisors and professionals, should all add this book to their libraries."

— S. Bryan Frazier, J.D., LL.M., Texas Estate and Elder Law Attorney

"I've worked with many people, but very few are consistently 'on-point' like Vincent is. Of all the professionals I have worked with in my life, I know he will get it right the first time and completely protect me and my family. He is incredibly fair, exhibits much integrity, and adroitly deals with the other professionals involved toward a successful resolution. Any book that explains the parameters of this practice is a book worth having in your library."

— Robert D. Liberti, Computer Science Engineer, Real Estate Investor

"In representing me as a fiduciary, Vincent always was calm and methodical despite the chaos and shenanigans of others in the probate matter. He always saw through the fog and was able to cut to the chase to get to resolution. In his book, as well, he brings this straightforward approach to simplify otherwise complicated matters."

— Wayne Palmer, Retired Automobile Body Shop Owner, Maple Syrup Producer

"Attorney Liberti is a dedicated and diligent estate planning attorney who finds creative solutions to best serve his clients. His book is an ideal read for anyone from a novice to a well-seasoned expert. His work addresses a variety of subjects, from Estate Planning and Trusts to Elder Law and Medicaid. Anyone interested in learning about these subjects, securing their financial health, and protecting their wealth would benefit from reading his book."

— Matthew T. Stillman, J.D., LL.M., Connecticut, Massachusetts, and New York Estate and Elder Law Attorney, Professor, Accredited Veterans Benefits Attorney, Former President Connecticut NAELA

"I met Vincent fifteen years ago at the first in the country LL.M. Program at Western New England University for Estate Planning and Elder Law. From the time I met him, Vincent demonstrated his relentless desire to know the material in each class, not just to get by, but to learn the material deeply and every nuance. Now, after being a practicing attorney for nearly thirty years and a law professor at that very LL.M. program for over a decade, Vincent can add 'author' to his many accomplishments. To this day, he answers every call and every email with trademark depth, empathy, and a sincere desire to solve the question or problem presented. This book is a synthesis of Vincent's professional career, infused with his unique ability to truly care for his students, colleagues, clients, and now his readers."

— Jeff Leland, J.D., LL.M. Massachusetts Estate and Elder Law Attorney

"Vincent has been a colleague and a friend for nearly a decade. I was first drawn to him by his easygoing manner and lack of pretentiousness. I soon learned these pleasant attributes overlay a formidable intellect and a complete mastery of elder law and estate planning. He is one of those rare attorneys who does not feel the need to immediately inform you of his profession or impress you with his knowledge; he would rather have a heartfelt conversation about the things that matter—family, friends, and good times. That said, when it is time to get down to the business of estate planning, he is truly without peer. I heartily recommend his book to anyone with the need to plan for future life events, which, of course, includes us all."

— Alan Curto, Pharmacist, Connecticut Attorney

"I was introduced to Attorney Liberti several years ago by trusted associates, first to handle my brother's estate and then to review and update my own estate plan. I was immediately impressed with his expertise and that he spent the time to listen and understand me, my family, and my business. He is thorough, thoughtful, and always quick to respond to questions or concerns. Vin's sense of humor always makes interactions enjoyable. I highly recommend his services."

— Tom McDowell, Owner of Connecticut Wedding Group, LLC and Pavilion Catering, LLC

"Vincent offers a thoughtful, detailed analysis of the myriad financial, legal, and emotional issues many people confront as they age, and how to prepare for them, especially in the latter stages of life. His comprehensive guide touches upon virtually every scenario an elder could face. I highly recommend this book to anyone concerned with educating themselves on elder planning issues."

— John D. Shea, J.D., LL.M., Massachusetts Estate & Asset Protection Planning Attorney

"A book long overdue! Attorney Vincent Liberti, Jr., LL.M. has labored over and created a piece of work that is a must read for all who labor. He has applied his education, vast experience in probate and finance, communication skills, and life experience to clearly and concisely educate everyone who reads it. It addresses areas that are so important but often overlooked or neglected until it is too late in life to reverse the damage. His cogent style has resulted in a bible providing financial and economic guidance to be followed throughout all phases of one's life to ensure there will be sufficient assets available at the end of our labors."

— Hon. Patricia L. Damon, Judge of the Connecticut Probate Court, Retired

"Vincent Liberti proves himself a knowledgeable and invaluable resource to everyone who needs to plan for end-of-life concerns. In *Preparing for Your Elder Years,* he offers practical and easy-to-understand information on everything you need to know about wills and trusts, long-term care, Medicare, and Medicaid, and much more. You'll feel empowered and reassured by this book and be able to make the best decisions throughout your life and leave a legacy."

— Patrick Snow, Publishing Coach and International Best-Selling Author of *Creating Your Own Destiny* and *Boy Entrepreneur*

"*Preparing for Your Elder Years* is a valuable resource about how to take care of your assets. Whether you are in your golden years, part of the Sandwich Generation worrying about how to care for elderly parents, or a young person who wants to make sure you're saving enough for retirement, you will find attorney Vincent Liberti's easy-to-read style and clear instructions a godsend."

— Tyler R. Tichelaar, PhD and Award-Winning Author of *Narrow Lives* and *The Best Place*

THE COMPLETE GUIDE TO CREATING SECURITY FOR YOUR (AND YOUR LOVED ONE'S) SENIOR YEARS

PREPARING FOR YOUR ELDER YEARS

TAKING CHARGE OF ESTATE PLANNING, LONG-TERM CARE, ASSET PROTECTION, AND MEDICAID

VINCENT LIBERTI, J.D., LL.M.

FOREWORD BY HYMAN G. DARLING

AVIVA PUBLISHING
New York

ACKNOWLEDGMENTS

I would like to acknowledge the following family, friends, mentors, and coaches who have impacted and supported me throughout my life:

Armen A. Abrahamian
Tammy Aiello
Samuel Allende
Jeffrey/Janice Alpert
Robert Anastasio
Carolyn Anderson
William G. Backer
Brent Berti
Joseph Biraglia
Richard Borer
Kevin Boykin
Terri Boyko
Lisa J. Cappalli
Americo R. Carchia
Frank Caruso
Thomas Cavaliere
Lisa A. Cerbone
Lillie Chandra
Stuart Clark
Joseph Collier
Maria Conlon
Mildred L. Corey
Michael Crowe
Alan Curto
Patricia L. Damon
Hyman G. Darling
Mark DeGennaro
Philip DeJesus
Lynn DeJoseph
William Donaldson
Kevin Doyle
John Dusza
Joseph Elhajj
Louis Elmo
Brian Enright
James Esposito
William P. Fauzio
Debra Fielden

Jean Fischer
Michael Forni
Duncan Forsyth
Joseph Fortner
S. Bryan Frazier
Elena Goggin
Pierre Guigui
Silvia N. Guinan
James S. Halligan
Casey Hoban
Paul G. Holland
Jason Howey
Drew Iacovazzi
David Jepson
Christopher Jones
Paul Kaplan
Susan Klaus
William Leavitt
Jacqueline Voss Lees
Jeffrey Leland
Mark F. Levesque
Charles Liberti
Brian Lindenberg
Michael Maddelena
Flo Aeveia Magdalena
James Maher
Nicholas Mancuso
Mark Marieb
Joseph Marino
Frank Mascia
Thomas Mason
Matthieu J. Massengill
Thomas McDowell
Kevin McNalley
Bennie Medina
Ralph A. Minichino
Nancy Moon
Richard/Ellen Moore
Richard Moran
Michael Mulcare
Tammy Napoli
Roberta L. Nestor
James Nugent
Joseph P. Nuzzo
Andrea Obston
Carrie O'Neil
Chanel Ostasiewski
Glenn Paddock
Christopher Pantani
Kelley Galicia Peck
Ida Colon-Perez
Thomas J. Perrone

Caleb M. Pilgrim
Andrew Pomfret
Louis Pontillo
Denise S. Popagoda
Mark Port
Anthony Raccio
William M. Raccio
Paul Raczynski
Robyn Vartelas Reilly
Paul/Trish Rhoda
Gary M. Richetelli
Dawn Robinson
Carmen Romano
Mary Jo Romano
Jay Rothman
Frederick D. Royal
Scott Sandler
Paul Sapiro
William Schaeneman
Andrew Schaffer
Suzanne Scibilia
Shirley Schiller
Julie Schlessel
David Sfara
John Shea
Jeffrey Shoemate
Mark Shumilla
Tad Smith
Filomena M. Soyster
Nicholas Stamboulis
Ned Steiger
Matthew Stillman
Brian Stone
Michael Strouch
Timothy Taylor
Terry T. Terzakis
Robert Testa
Tavis Tindall
Daniel Tomassini
Frederick Trotta
Earl Tucker
Kenneth Tullo
Thomas A. Virgulto
Adam Westphalen
Roni S. White
Andrew Worthington
Michael Wrona
Pearl Wynkoop

SPECIAL ACKNOWLEDGMENTS

Sincere appreciation and a special thank you to Armen Abrahamian, Alan Curto, Hyman G. Darling, Jeffrey Leland, Paul Liberti, Kelley Galicia Peck, Patrick Snow, and Matthew Stillman for graciously spending time reviewing my grammar and content, and providing valuable advice, and to all those wonderful friends and clients who provided such kind and humbling testimonials of me and this book. No individual is an island; without all of you, this project would not be a success. Thank you.

FOREWORD

In the beginning of my career as an elder law attorney, I learned that successful lawyers know how to communicate complicated legal matters effectively. Then, as my career progressed, I learned how rewarding it is to truly connect to others in the process. I met "Vinny" when he was my student in the LL.M. (Master of Laws) program at Western New England University School of Law. Almost immediately, we developed a good rapport. He, too, has learned the techniques of successful communication and the rewards of connecting with others. I never anticipated that so many years later, he would become a prolific writer and give me the honor of writing a foreword to his book.

This book is a wonderful roadmap of knowledge for learning estate planning options, achieving financial goals, accumulating and sheltering wealth, and preserving such wealth for yourself and your family's future generations. From housing to long-term care and from tax issues to protecting wealth, Vincent has demonstrated his expansive knowledge and provided a clear and concise path for you to follow for your planning. Whether saving estate taxes or applying for Medicaid for long-term care services, you will learn specific knowledge and skills to build your security through a well-organized and clear analysis with detailed and organized suggestions. You probably will wish to go back and read a chapter more than once to educate yourself on questions you should ask your accountant, lawyer, or financial advisor. Through Vincent's powerful book, you will learn to spot the key issues to protect yourself and your family, whether your spouse, sibling, or parent, and know when to take the necessary actions before it is too late.

In *Preparing for Your Elder Years*, Vincent empowers you to take control of your financial and physical health, especially for your senior years. Allow him to be the driver in your life so you may pursue the path toward your security and whatever is necessary for you to determine through this amazing journey.

Hyman G. Darling, Estate Planning and Elder Law Attorney, Former President of the National Academy of Elder Law Attorneys (NAELA). Adjunct Professor of Law, Western New England University, LL.M. Program, Certified Elder Law Attorney by the National Elder Law Foundation

INTRODUCTION

STARTING THE JOURNEY TOWARD PEACE OF MIND

"By failing to prepare, you are preparing to fail."

— Benjamin Franklin

Much is written about creating your nest egg for retirement. A rule of thumb is to invest enough for you to live at least comfortably by withdrawing about 4 percent annually from retirement funds, combined with Social Security benefits, and perhaps a pension. This book will focus on planning for issues beyond mere retirement, yet as you shall see, many people under-invest for even their basic retirement needs. As a result, too many of my senior clients are terribly surprised when confronted with expenses associated with long-term care, including Medicaid spend-down planning. Are you prepared for a debilitating event in your later years? Do you appreciate how this unpreparedness not only affects your life, but also the lives of your spouse and family? This book provides a picture of such issues, encourages you to conduct an honest appraisal of your own situation, and provides you with choices to create a different path for yourself. From my perspective, a crisis of individual unpreparedness exists that is causing an increasing collective cost to loved ones and society. The good news is we can do something about it.

After almost three decades of handling estate planning and elder matters, I increasingly encounter a rather typical situation with my elder clients. They abruptly learn too late the path they could have taken to be better prepared for a debilitating event in the latter stage of their lives, which I refer to in this book as an "End-Stage" event. This situation is well-known to people who privately have experienced a loved one's End-Stage event, but such matters are seldom addressed publicly. I see an overwhelming gap in our American lives that leaves seniors, especially senior women, unprepared for such debilitating events. Adding to the problem, as all of us get older, and particularly after an End-Stage event, we become a bit confused with handling money, or even a little paranoid of others (even family members) who offer their help. Conversely, we may become increasingly reliant upon certain family members, helpful neighbors, or even outsiders, attracting the risk of financial fraud, or worse, physical abuse. Have you developed a proper estate plan, especially to appoint key people to make medical and financial decisions for you when you cannot, in case of an End-Stage event?

The most disheartening moment in representing such clients is when a spouse, typically the wife, confronts the complexity and expense of dealing with an End-Stage event that has just befallen her partner. Most often, the spouse or loved one must quickly learn about these matters and other End-Stage issues discussed in this book from their lawyer, and at considerable expense. Many areas are involved when handling an End-Stage event, so both broad and specific education are needed to achieve more security in your life. Do you understand financial matters well enough to produce the wealth to protect yourself and your partner? How well might you handle the complicated bureaucracy of government programs, long-term care issues, and Medicaid?

To help present these many End-Stage issues, I will first introduce you to a senior client named Ellen, who has to deal with her husband Bob's End-Stage event and then her own potential declining faculties. Although Ellen's scenario may be more typical of today's unprepared seniors, you may avoid this path with a little knowledge and preparedness. As we shall see, the earlier you alter this typical path, the better and easier it is to create security for your later years.

I repeatedly experience this gap in preparedness dealing

with End-Stage issues and inform those who take the time to educate themselves about it, but the threshold question remains: If you could go back in time and reveal to your younger self the course you then were on and where it leads, would the younger you put less emphasis on present comfort, and more emphasis on preparing for the financial costs of your later years, and in particular, End-Stage issues? Would you choose to conscientiously change your financial decisions and have the discipline not to be swayed by the cacophony of advertising and marketing that seeks to convince you that the mere appearance of wealth constitutes the living of the American Dream? In other words, would you create your own security for your later years? My most heart-wrenching experiences are watching not only clients but also my own family members fail to prepare and then suffer the consequences. This book not only provides a picture of End-Stage issues, but also shows you how to create the necessary security to avoid them.

I begin in Chapter One by presenting Ellen's factual scenario. We will revisit her situation throughout this book after introducing certain financial concepts necessary to understand the topics presented later. I also introduce and define financial and estate planning ideas. In Chapter Two about wealth and finances, I refer to the conclusions of the book *The Millionaire Next Door,*[1] and I suggest you refer to its message on who builds wealth in the United States, their habits, and emotional relationship with money and wealth. Although you may think these millionaires lead lives that are too frugal for you, observing their behaviors may paint a vision of a more sensible lifestyle. An absolute necessity for preparing for your End-Stage issues is knowing the amount of wealth (not just income), needed for each stage of your life in order to establish and maintain a comfortable standard of living to the end. The financial ideas are of budgets, the time-value of money, assumption of liability and protection costs (such as those associated with accident, death, and long-term care needs), transfer of liability risk (to insurance companies), and investment scenarios for each life cycle. These core principles are essential to understand to create your End-Stage security. I also present the necessary strategies to protect your wealth, starting with general estate planning and asset protection considerations and ending with options for sheltering high levels of wealth. Asset protection and estate planning concepts discussed include medical and financial directives/proxies/powers, last wills and testaments, trusts, and other options to hold and shelter wealth, along with the many traps and misconceptions associated with these concepts. Throughout this book, I revisit estate planning options with each topic or challenging stage of your life being discussed.

The knowledge in this book presents you with a clear picture of the many factors affecting the creation and protection of your wealth for the type of End-Stage security you choose to create. Above all, while knowledge is key, your having the necessary attitude to choose the right course of action is critical.

Next, I discuss illness and long-term care (LTC) matters, followed by a discussion on ideas for how to prepare for End-Stage issues during each life stage, such as: 1) your first job, 2) marriage, 3) having children, 4) divorce, and 5) retirement. In each stage is a discussion of suggested financial and estate (asset protection) planning actions for building your security. This book is not a course in retirement planning, but rather a guide that provides you with intelligent financial, asset protection, and long-term care options to consider to maintain the comfortable life you desire, right to the end.

I then tackle elder financial abuse concerns, long-term care insurance, and housing issues for your later years. Next is a discussion on spending down your assets to qualify for Medicaid assistance, family issues during an End-Stage event and after death, and estate planning suggestions to avoid them. Before concluding, I provide a chapter on the financial burdens of the Medicaid program from the federal and the state perspective.

Financial planners provide help with your savings and investments. For estate planning, asset protection, and Medicaid planning, an attorney is necessary. Healthcare professionals and government agencies provide additional help with long-term care matters. However, many of us do not have financial planners, and even fewer have one who fully understands our investment needs throughout life's various stages, especially the later years. Financial planners who do have this expertise tend to focus on clients with higher levels of investable wealth. For instance, when the economy is doing well, I often hear that these financial planners only take new clients with $500,000, $750,000, or more, to invest, although during recessionary times, these amounts tend to be lower.

Local banks may appear to be a source of investment options for people of modest means; however, banks view investment advice chiefly as an additional profit center, so their investment advisors tend to be primarily salespeople with limited financial knowledge and few investment options to offer you. Perhaps, in time, artificial intelligence may advance to the point where individuals with modest investable wealth will have access to the current human acumen necessary to invest properly, and perhaps at a cheaper cost. However, society is not there yet. The fact remains that at present, unless you have sufficient wealth to attract a highly qualified financial planner, you likely are not fully informed on how to adequately protect yourself financially throughout your life.

Lawyers, too, are not all the same. The friendly lawyer who helped you purchase your home may not be the best person to adequately advise you beyond a simple will or a standardized power of attorney, and he or she may not be aware of the many issues involved with such documents. In addition, many generalist lawyers cannot adequately adapt an estate plan to changing circumstances throughout your life. With respect to an End-Stage event, you need specialized legal expertise, particularly to understand the difference between Medicare and Medicaid coverage, how to protect assets, and how to pay for End-Stage illnesses. If you have had inadequate legal support, once an End-Stage event occurs such as a stroke, or the onset of dementia, a basic estate plan may be not only inadequate, but also beyond correction even by a skilled attorney.

As an attorney who has practiced almost exclusively in the area of estate planning and elder law for nearly three decades, even earning an advanced law degree in estate planning and elder law, I continually learn more and better ways to help my clients. Prior to law school, I obtained my Bachelor of Science in Industrial Economics. With knowledge and compassion, I use my education and experience to help my clients achieve the two goals they all hope to accomplish, and with reasonable health, preparation, and a bit of luck, we all have an opportunity to achieve. These two goals are maintaining your accustomed standard of living throughout retirement and providing for your loved ones after you are gone. Ironically, given our almost universal desire to achieve these goals, too many of us fail to do the things needed to accomplish them. The reason is not difficult to understand. Many people do not wish to confront the universal fact of our eventual old age and mortality, so they put off planning for them. Additionally, our most pressing need throughout the majority of our lives is to deal with the here and now (and the exigencies we inevitably encounter, such as job change or loss, college expenses for children, and other financial pressures, foreseen and unforeseen), which often results in our losing sight of the need to plan for ourselves. Although there is no silver bullet for success and the law is constantly changing, my experience and knowledge, as shared in the following pages, will fully inform you so you will find your path to success.

In short, this book will educate you about, and inform you on, financial, estate planning, and long-term care matters (especially Medicaid issues) so you are protected for the economic, asset protection, and health decisions during your life, especially in your later years. I seek to empower you to be in control of these matters throughout your life. The implementation of the necessary steps, of course, is up to you. As the adage says, there is no time like the present, and given the time it takes to gracefully build your End-Stage security, the sooner you start your journey, the better!

CHAPTER ONE:

SEEING THE INDIVIDUAL FOCUS—THE CASE OF ELLEN

"Prepare the umbrella before it rains."

— Malay Proverb

I am having my initial meeting with Ellen, who has been referred to me by her neighbor, a life-care planner. Overwhelmed, confused, and saddened, Ellen went to her neighbor for help after her husband suffered a stroke. Understanding the difficult course Ellen now is on, the planner referred her to me to review her (and her husband's) estate planning preparedness, analyze their financial needs going forward given the added costs involved, and explain the many issues she will have to tackle, including how Medicare and Medicaid work.

Ellen is seventy-nine years old and looks a bit disheveled in appearance. Her energy seems low. Her voice is slow and strained.

As she speaks, I notice her posture is slumped rather than upright and positive. Her husband, Bob (age eighty-one), has been in the hospital since his stroke. The doctors have determined that Bob is unable to manage his medical decisions or his financial affairs. He has stabilized, but he will require rehabilitation before walking again, hopefully on his own someday. His mental and physical health have drastically changed.

In our meeting, I learn that Ellen and Bob have been married for more than fifty years, have enjoyed a comfortable life, and have managed their lives together fine. They have a nice home with a small amount of mortgage debt remaining, cars that are decent if a bit old, modest investments, and grown children who are busy raising their own families, although Ellen likes to help them financially now and then. In short, Ellen and Bob are a rather typical older couple.

However, Ellen has now been told that she does not have written authority to make medical decisions for Bob; to do so, she may have to go to probate court to obtain a guardian (conservator) appointment. Furthermore, their bank will not allow Ellen to access any accounts in Bob's name only. Additionally, after reviewing Ellen and Bob's estate planning documents, I sadly had to inform her that they are outdated and too simplistic, and, therefore, inadequate for their present needs. Bob and Ellen had never executed the legal documents necessary to appoint each other to handle their respective medical and financial affairs, which has now resulted in Ellen's lacking legal authority to handle such matters for Bob.

In addition, a nurse has informed Ellen that at some point Bob's Medicare benefits will end, so she must prepare to handle where he will live and how to pay for his care and living arrangements. Ellen wishes to have Bob return home, although she understands that first he must stay at a rehabilitation facility. Ellen was provided with facility options for Bob's rehabilitation. The nurse also explained a home assessment must be done before Bob can go home after rehabilitation to determine if the house is safe for Bob, given his condition. No facility will release him home unless it is determined that it is safe for Bob and Ellen has the physical and mental ability to tend to Bob's ambulatory, cognitive, and medical needs. Many people, including friends and hospital staff, have attempted to help Ellen, but their advice has often been conflicting and confusing for Ellen.

After discussing their income and expenses, their family history (including longevity), and her wishes for Bob's care, Ellen firmly states that she wants Bob home; she is dead set against his living apart from her in some facility after so many years living together. With these wishes in mind, Ellen and I assess whether she can afford a 24/7 home-care aide, along with the home renovations costs necessary for Bob to be released home.

I next have to inform Ellen that Medicare benefits are only for healthcare costs for people age sixty-five and older and do not cover long-term care issues. With respect to Bob, once his recovery plateaus, and his care transitions to help with cognitive abilities or with activities of daily living (such as transporting, eating, bathing, etc.), Medicare coverage ceases, so Ellen will have to pay for his care either by: 1) self-paying, 2) long-term care insurance, or 3) spending down assets and applying for Medicaid—a joint federal and state "safety net" program for those in need of financial assistance with long-term care costs.

I advise Ellen that to qualify for Medicaid in her state, assets in Bob's name must be valued at no greater than $2,000 (in other states $1,600). Her assets will also be affected. Ellen will be allowed to keep assets in her name worth up to a certain cap or limit in value (again, varying by state of application). For Ellen, this limit is just over $126,000. She also must account for the last five years—the look-back period—of her and Bob's finances and assets. If Ellen and Bob gifted assets within this period, they will have a disqualifying period of Medicaid coverage. Ellen, although a bit frail, is a healthy seventy-nine-year-old. She has longevity in her family history—her father lived to eighty-eight and her mother to ninety-three—although her mother had some dementia in her later years, as did some other family members.

The sudden decrease in Ellen's accustomed lifestyle, modest as it is, as well as the prospect of such limited funds with which to survive, gravely concerns her. Her new responsibilities as to Bob's care needs are also weighing heavily upon her. As a result, she has become distraught to the point of near-paralysis with decision-making. She is genuinely concerned about how she will provide, not just for Bob, but for herself going forward.

Before Bob's stroke, Ellen had assumed she and Bob would continue to enjoy their lives, help their children and grandchildren financially on occasion, and travel for as long as they could. All that now has suddenly changed, and she is starting to realize their life will never be the same. Ellen turns to me and says, "I wish I had known all of these things you have just explained to me a long time ago. I do not seem to have any good choices. What do I do now?"

Ellen's situation is not uncommon. What if you are on the same path as Ellen? This book's purpose is to describe the many issues Ellen may have wanted to know "a long time ago" for you to be better prepared. Her journey, however, was not over; the following scenario illustrates additional issues with seniors also discussed in this book.

A few years later, after Bob passed, I receive a call from Ellen's care planner-neighbor, who explains that a few months ago, Ellen was in the hospital because she had fallen and broken her hip. She did rehabilitation and recently returned home, yet she did not appear to be quite the same and now even seemed to be more forgetful. Yesterday, the neighbor had a conversation with Ellen, who explained that her daughter and son-in-law wished to move in to help take care of her. Ellen wants to have a new financial power of attorney drafted to have just her daughter as her agent, which Ellen describes as "to better take care of her." Having spent a lot of time getting to know Ellen's family after Bob had his stroke, the care planner is concerned with Ellen's new reliance on her daughter and son-in-law. The care planner explains that previously Ellen had said her husband never totally trusted their daughter's husband, who seemed not to stay in the same employment for long and frequently changed types of jobs. He and Ellen's daughter do not seem to manage their finances well, always seeming to need money. Bob had complained that they provided financial assistance to them disproportionately to what they provided to their other children. Ellen also explained that her son-in-law wished to invest her remaining investments for her to make a higher rate of return, even though he is not a licensed financial planner, nor has any investment experience. The care planner believes Ellen is financially at risk and needs help.

After a lengthy conversation with the care planner, I agree that Ellen may be at financial risk, especially given her lack of experience handling finances, her apparent forgetfulness, and her newfound reliance on her daughter and son-in-law. I agree to contact Ellen to discuss her desire to create a new power of attorney and simultaneously assess her mental capacity to do so. I assume her daughter will be with her for the visit. While they are in my office, I will observe any dependence Ellen has on her daughter and son-in-law and try to determine if any abuse is occurring—financially, physically, or mentally. In addition, Ellen may soon need to apply for Medicaid assistance, depending upon her future needs. If she gifts assets to her daughter, such gifting may harm her chances for Medicaid eligibility. Her daughter's management of Ellen's funds also may negatively impact Ellen's eligibility for Medicaid.

PREPAREDNESS QUESTIONS

1. What plans have you made to prepare for an End-Stage event for you or your partner?

2. Which estate planning documents do you require in case you become incapacitated? Have you executed them, and are they current?

3. If dementia is a hereditary trait in your family, what measures have you taken to prepare for your potential dementia?

4. Who are your go-to people in case of a debilitating event?

CHAPTER TWO:

UNDERSTANDING KEY CONCEPTS OF WEALTH, INVESTMENTS, AND ASSET PROTECTION

"...the best possible way to prepare for tomorrow is to concentrate with all your intelligence, all your enthusiasm, on doing today's work superbly today. That is the only possible way you can prepare for the future."

— Dale Carnegie, *How to Stop Worrying and Start Living*

Before discussing specific elder issues in subsequent chapters, this chapter presents basic, yet important, financial concepts on how to build and manage wealth. These concepts are core principles to understand for how to create your End-Stage security and gracefully build a different scenario to that of Ellen's in the last chapter. The next chapter will discuss estate planning and asset protection concepts, which will be discussed throughout this book, so you can know how to protect such security. This chapter's building wealth concepts are fundamental matters dealing with budgeting, investing, debt management, wealth, and types of insurance protection, for not only End-Stage issues, but your entire life.

LEARNING INCOME, EXPENSES, AND WEALTH

1. **Income:** Generally, income is defined as money, property,[2] or services received from work or investments. However, there are many different concepts for income. Income is more expansive than just earned income such as that from a salary, wages, bonuses, tips on services, or self-employment, which are considered taxable income. According to the Internal Revenue Code (IRC), gross income is all income from whatever source derived, such as from compensation, business income, gains (dealing with property), interest, rents, royalties, dividends, alimony payments, annuities, pensions, forgiveness of a debt owed, etc.

   It may be taxable[3] or non-taxable. For it to be non-taxable, it must be exempt from income in the IRC. Examples of non-taxable income are welfare, unemployment, and worker's compensation. Adjusted Gross Income, or AGI, is taxable income after the application of permissible deductions and credits. AGI is the figure you use to determine your income taxes, yet it is not exactly what we would consider take-home pay or the income we use to pay our expenses.

For our discussion, especially when creating a budget, the business concept of "net income," meaning gross revenue minus operating (home) expenses, may be a better concept to use for what we consider as usable income, which is money available to you to handle your home expenses and investments. Net income would simply be our gross income minus deductions and taxes. Income, or net income, may be used interchangeably in this book, but the meaning is the amount of income available to you after taxes for your expenses, savings, and investments. Do not, however, confuse income with wealth.

2. **Expenses:** Personal expenses are closely related to our spending. Expenses may be more fixed, such as rent payments or payments to your lender on the promissory note (or IOU) that you give to a lender[4] in order to buy your home, other loans such as student loans and auto loans, health insurance costs, daycare, tuition, and basic utilities. Variable, also called discretionary, expenses are those obligations you have more choice on whether to incur, and if so, how much you pay for them. Variable expenses could be further divided into necessary variable expenses (or

partially discretionary expenses) that provide a basic comfort in life that you may deem you need, and fully discretionary expenses, which you could do without. Partially discretionary expenses might involve types of groceries, home and car maintenance, clothing, or the amount/usage of electric/heating/air-conditioning expenses. For these expenses, you have a choice of how comfortable you choose to be given the cost for the comfort. When making such choices, you can apply a cost/benefit or need/want analysis. Fully discretionary expenses may be eating out, certain clothing expenses, hobbies, entertainment, gift giving, travel, and other "luxury" items. However, do not totally disregard these items. Plan them as a reward for yourself, perhaps for maintaining your established budget. Create in your budget a percentage to save for these personal rewards.

3. **Wealth and Net Worth:** Personal (economic) wealth, in general, is the value of all you own—savings, investments, equity in our home, cash, etc. Net worth is your wealth less your debts (all you owe). According to the book *The Millionaire Next Door*, at any given time your net worth should be your gross income (pre-tax income) times your age, divided by 10.

$$\frac{(\text{Income}) \times (\text{Age})}{10} = \text{Personal Wealth}$$

For instance, assuming an average individual in the United States has a gross annual income of $69,000 and is thirty years of age, given this formula, such an individual's personal wealth should be $207,000. (The Federal Reserve Bank of New York reports an average U.S. income of $69,181 as of November 2019.) Notice that this definition does not include in the equation a variable called "When I have no debt, then I'll invest." Although paying down debt is a priority, the longer you wait to invest, the greater the loss of the benefit of compound returns (see time-value of money section following). Also, note that for a married couple, the term household wealth often is used, which means net worth of the family. Many people confuse income with wealth; they are not the same. While very few people have achieved wealth overnight, the overwhelming majority create wealth over time, with a clear, disciplined plan to achieve it. Unfortunately, the overwhelming public message in the United States is about those who achieve wealth (or perhaps just high income) overnight and very seldom about those who create it through good habits and discipline over time.

DEVELOPING A PERSONAL BUDGET

A personal budget is the careful accounting of your income and expenses. The more exact and honest you are with your expenses, habits, and desires, the better the budget. Start with gross income, and subtract federal, state, and local taxes, FICA, Medicare, and other payroll deductions to obtain net income. Other deductions to subtract from gross income may be health costs, or 401(k) contributions, which should be accounted for separately.

On the expense side, consider grouping them according to fixed expenses or needs, and variable expenses, which can be subcategorized into partially variable expenses and fully discretionary or luxury expenses. With honest analysis of needs versus wants, you can devise a balanced personal budget that incorporates living for today and planning for tomorrow. Some fixed expense items may have discretionary choices within them. Examples are the type of food you buy or the television/cable/internet package you purchase.

A sample monthly budget has the following categories. A simple notebook or MS Excel compilation may work quite fine, although computer programs such as Quicken also assist with compiling a budget. Your budget does not end with just income and expense items. Leave room for investments and savings, including an emergency fund. The more you limit expenses, especially discretionary ones, the more you will have to save and invest, and the greater financial security you will create. As we shall see, this financial security affects your quality of life, especially in your later years, which is a theme of this book—your End-Stage security.

Gross Income:

Add all sources of income

Subtract: Federal Income Tax, State Income Tax, Local Income Tax, FICA

(Social Security) and Medicare:

Other deductions (not separately accounted for elsewhere in budget)

Equals - Net Income:

Expenses:

Fixed:

Housing (Mortgage or Rent):

Homeowner/Renter's Insurance:

Property Taxes:

Condo Fees:

Utilities:

Food:

Tuition:

Loans (School, Car, other):

Variable:

Daycare:

Repairs/Improvements – home & car:

Health/Dental Insurance, co-pays, uninsured costs:

Emergency Savings Fund:

Transportation, Gas:

Non-Qualified Savings/Investments:

Other such variable expenses:

Discretionary:

Coffee purchases:

Gym/Fitness:

Eating out:

Entertainment:

Club membership:

Subscriptions:

Vacations:

Other:

Investments

401(k):

Other investments:

Savings/money market:

Checking account:

Emergency fund:

When making a budget given your life choices, consider the following budgeting parameters. Determine your priorities accordingly.

1. **Emergency Fund:** Establish an emergency fund to weather the storm in case of unforeseen negative financial circumstances, such as with your vehicle, furnace, water heater, roof, and other needed mechanicals that may fail or need repair; unemployment; a virus pandemic; etc. You never know when your financial health may be at risk. Besides creating peace of mind, an emergency fund will prevent your creating debt through borrowing needed funds at an extra cost of interest. It also assists with issues of disability and ensuing time off from work, as well as such time in-between jobs. The benefit is not just financial. Having the peace of mind to know you can handle whatever financial challenge you may encounter also helps your emotional health. To determine your emergency fund amount, one rule of thumb is to eliminate the taxes and payroll contributions you otherwise would pay without loss of work from an emergency, investments, and luxury items, to determine your basic income need in case of an emergency. Then establish in your budget an emergency fund savings amount to build up at least 3-6 months of such expenses, perhaps longer, especially if you do not have disability insurance or if you have a family dependent upon your income.

2. **Debt Management:** Next, consider debt management. Whether considering the purchase of a home, tuition costs, or credit for needed expense items, seek only to incur debt for large purchases that create equity. Credit cards debt should only be used for convenience and paid back as soon as possible to avoid interest charges; otherwise, avoid using credit cards. Certainly, do not use credit card debt to support a lifestyle you otherwise cannot afford. If you must incur debt, optimally seek to keep it under 20 percent of your net income, especially in your early years of life. Plan to eliminate all debts as quickly as possible and especially upon retiring. However, if you choose to incur debt, consider the following parameters, which generally are financing guidelines.

3. **Mortgage Debt Ratio:** When you decide to purchase a home, calculate your expected mortgage debt—your mortgage payments composed of Principal and Interest, Property Taxes, and Homeowner's Insurance (referred to as PITI)—and divide it by your monthly gross income. This quotient should be less than or equal to 28 percent of your net income. Then consider your non-mortgage debt-to-income ratio.

4. **Non-Mortgage Debt-to-Income Ratio:** Your non-mortgage debt-to-income ratio is your annual (non-mortgage) debt payments divided by your annual net income. This other debt may be payments on loans, credit cards, monthly expenses,

etc. The ratio should be no greater than 15 percent of your net income.

5. **Monthly Debt-to-Income Ratio:** The monthly debt-to-income ratio is your monthly PITI + monthly (other) debt, divided by gross monthly income. Keep this ratio less than or equal to 36 percent.

6. **Savings:** Establish savings initially between 10 and 15 percent of your gross income.

7. **Investments:** Any remaining net income after all expenses and savings should be invested, although the first objective should be managing debt and expenses to create (and increase) your investing percentage. Advice is varied on how much one should invest. With tighter budgets, especially when new to the job market and strapped by student loans, 10 percent of your net income may be appropriate. Seek to increase it to a healthier 20 percent (or higher), continually increasing it as you pay down your debt and as you age. If you work for an employer that matches your retirement account (generally a 401(k), which is usually capped at a certain amount), seek to invest at least the maximum amount to add this employer wealth to your retirement investments. Review the section of this chapter on time-value-of-money to understand the importance of this added benefit. Be mindful of the

loss you will incur the longer you wait to invest. Establish a balanced budget from the start of your career to create and maintain your financial security.

8. **College Planning:** A rule of thumb for investing in a child's college tuition is about 5 percent of your annual net income. See Chapter Five for other considerations with college choices.

UNDERSTANDING INSURANCE AND TRANSFERRING RISK OF LOSS

For some risk of loss, the law imposes that you must obtain insurance to mitigate or pay in full the costs incurred. Automobile insurance is one such type of government-imposed insurance. Health insurance under the Affordable Care Act[5] was an attempt at another government-imposed insurance. Other insurance is optional, and it can be difficult to determine whether it is needed, and if so, how much. When determining whether to insure someone, insurance companies look at: 1) Risk, which involves the possibility of loss; 2) Peril, which involves the cause of the loss; and 3) Hazard, which involves the increased potential for loss. Thus, determining whether to obtain insurance involves an assessment of the probability of risk, the frequency of the activity that gives rise to such risk, and the financial loss when it occurs.

To understand this concept, it may be easiest to examine

extreme examples of risk. One extreme example is an activity with a high probability of loss with an exceedingly high frequency of the activity's occurrence, like auto racing. The other extreme is an activity with an extremely low probability of loss coupled with an exceptionally low frequency of occurrence. In the first case, reducing or avoiding such behavior may be the best choice; however, if you seek to continue the activity and transfer the risk of financial loss, seek insurance coverage. Certain activities representing the former scenario may involve an exceedingly high cost of insurance for that transfer of financial risk to the insurance company, or perhaps, no coverage if the activity is deemed too risky (to the insurance company). For the latter scenario, the financial loss has such a low probability, coupled with a low financial loss, that you likely would assume the financial cost of such activity. The difficulty, then, is choosing to insure for activities and their potential losses that lie between these two extremes. Working with a good insurance agent will assist you in determining the cost to insure certain activities or occurrences to determine whether it is preferable to self-pay for the loss or shift that burden to an insurance company. A healthy emergency fund may also dissuade the need to transfer certain risk.

1. **Umbrella Policy:** In some cases, you may wish to obtain extra liability insurance over and above regular casualty insurance, such as homeowners, auto, and boat insurance. This extra

type of insurance coverage is called umbrella insurance, and it may cover claims excluded from regular coverage. It is designed to cover the insured against major claims (or lawsuits) to protect his or her assets. Therefore, it is a type of asset protection. Having a personal business or hobby, rental property, or even a child starting to drive are examples of situations for which you may want to look at an umbrella policy.

2. **Life Insurance:** Two issues surround life insurance: 1) determining the amount of life insurance desired, and 2) determining the type or types of life insurance to obtain. For individuals, generally life insurance is about your personal obligations and desires as well as family survival needs upon the death of the insured individual.

    a. **Determining amount of insurance:** A sample formula to determine the amount of life insurance for an individual might look like the following:

Amount of Life Insurance =

Liabilities (debt) + Replacement Income + Education Costs + Legacy + Burial Costs + Estate Taxes

You may choose to purchase life insurance to leverage debt and obligations that may exist at death to avoid burdening heirs with such debt. Likewise, you may wish to provide some insurance proceeds to assist the family with the loss of your income at death. For lost income, the idea is to at least help the surviving spouse/partner and/or family with enough time to "catch their breath" after losing not only a loved one but also your income (and service) contributions to the management of the household.

Loss of income may be easy to determine, but having one parent do what two used to do may entail extra costs to replace the services the decedent used to do, such as childcare, carpool duties, shopping, home repair, or even cooking. It also may involve increased income taxes due to filing as a single taxpayer instead of married on a joint income tax return. All these factors should be considered, then quantified. Quantifying the loss of income and/or help around the house may seem obvious, but what is not so obvious is that when someone loses a loved one, it takes time—approximately 1-2 years—for him or her to start thinking straight again and managing what once was handled by the person who now is gone. Replacing income through life insurance proceeds helps the survivor ease into the new role and adjust to the loss.

Education costs are that amount, if any, you choose

to pay for a child's tuition and other related expenses. Legacy is the amount you are willing to spend for increased life insurance coverage to provide inheritance to children and family. If you expect to incur estate taxes on death, life insurance is a good means to leverage such costs instead of depleting your estate assets to pay the tax. Lastly, the traditional idea of life insurance is to cover burial costs. Burial costs vary according to the region of the country, but if such costs are not too high, you simply may choose to incorporate the costs into savings/investments and thus retain that risk instead of transferring it to an insurance company through life insurance. In most states, pre-paying for burial costs is protected through statutory trusts (incorporating Medicaid concerns) that funeral homes create for a customer. These statutory trusts enable you to plan and pay for your burial costs in advance to unburden family members and avoid such life insurance costs.

This basic formula not only helps you assess the issues surrounding life insurance, but also your personal desires about each variable in order to obtain a rational determination of whether you need life insurance, and if so, how much. In many instances, it is desirable to layer different types of life insurance given the need for each variable. First, let us look at the different types of insurance before examining this layering concept.

b. **Types of life insurance:** Many types of life insurance policies exist, some designed to increase cash value, some as investment vehicles, and some simply to mitigate loss over a certain time frame. Some policies provide dividends that increase the life insurance death benefit or reduce the insurance premium. Some policies are single premium policies; others you pay as you go. Other policies are designed so you can borrow from the policy's cash value. It is essential to discuss your needs and the details of any proposed policy or policies with a good insurance agent or broker.

Traditional life insurance involved just term insurance and permanent insurance. Term insurance simply involves a guaranteed death benefit payout upon the death of the insured (person whose life is being insured) for a set period. Once the time period ends, the policy lapses and the death benefit ends. This type of insurance is likened to renting and is cheaper than permanent life insurance, which builds cash value.

Permanent insurance now comes in many forms, depending upon one's purpose for the insurance and price sensitivity. This type of insurance costs more than term insurance. Whole life is the most common type of permanent insurance. It generally involves a fixed premium throughout the policy, a guaranteed death benefit, and a guaranteed (minimum) cash value.

Sometimes, it may be advantageous to choose both term insurance and permanent insurance to create tiered levels of insurance coverage to accomplish specific goals during phases of life and to mitigate insurance costs. For instance, perhaps term insurance could be used to cover payments on a thirty-year mortgage or for college tuition expenses for children. When the need ends—the mortgage is paid off or the children have (should be) finished with college—life insurance is no longer needed for these debts or obligations. A term policy may be the simple solution to mitigate loss of death during these particular time frames of need. Alternatively, you may desire to build wealth through life insurance, or you may have life insurance needs for which a time frame cannot be easily determined. To save on insurance costs, permanent life insurance could be obtained for those specific needs in conjunction with term insurance instead of a larger, and more costly, permanent policy for all your insurance needs.

If you need life insurance to pay estate (death) taxes upon the death of the second spouse (see Chapter Three on estate planning), you may choose a type of permanent policy called a second-to-die policy, which only pays a death benefit when the second spouse dies. This policy usually costs less than two permanent policies on the life of each spouse.

c. **Long-Term Care:** Long-term care (LTC) insurance is probably the least known type of insurance, but for many, it may be the most important to have for an End-Stage event in your life. It is not disability insurance, but insurance designed to assist the insured with long-term care needs that health insurance does not cover. It differs from disability insurance, which is designed to provide income lost due to a short- or long-term disability. Although other categories of LTC coverage exist, skilled nursing, intermediate care, and custodial care are the three main levels. LTC insurance covers costs for the following services.

- Home care
- Adult day care
- Assisted living facility care
- Hospice care
- A nursing facility or long-term care facility

LTC provides insurance coverage for people who have impaired cognitive abilities (dementia) or require assistance with two or more activities of daily living (ADLs) for a minimum period of ninety days. ADLs involve activities dealing with the following.

- Bathing
- Continence
- Dressing
- Eating
- Toileting
- Transferring, such as from bed to sofa, or to bathroom[6]

Many people confuse Medicare with Medicaid. Medicare is health insurance, and it generally does not cover long-term care needs. Medicaid does, if one qualifies. See Chapters Four and Eight for a more detailed explanation of each program.

IDENTIFYING QUALIFIED AND NON-QUALIFIED INVESTMENTS

Qualified investments are those investments in which pre-tax income is used to contribute to a retirement plan. These investments are not subject to income taxes until you withdraw the funds. However, if you seek to withdraw funds before attaining age 59½, there is a 10 percent penalty. At age 72,[7] the government forces mandatory minimum withdrawals (Required Minimum Distributions, or RMDs, sometimes called Minimum Required Distributions, or MRDs). Examples of such investments are 401(k), 403(b), traditional IRA, certain annuities, and certain registered retirement savings plans (RRSP). The government sets limits on how much you may invest each year for these investments.

Non-Qualified investments are all other investments that have no income tax-deferral or tax-exempt status. Therefore, they require post-tax income for the investment, and the interest earned on the investment may be taxable income. This income is reported to the investment owner yearly on a form, 1099-NT. Examples of these investments are non-qualified annuities, mutual funds, stocks, bonds, savings accounts, certain precious metals, and art investments.

UNDERSTANDING BANK ACCOUNTS

A savings account or money market account is the simplest way to invest but at an extremely low rate of return. Some checking accounts bear interest, but again, at extremely low rates. Checking accounts are traditional convenient ways to pay for goods and services; however, for some people, a money market account is preferable to build more interest income. In general, these accounts are not good investments, but are for mere convenience when liquidity is desired. They also involve little risk of loss.

LEARNING ABOUT RATE OF RETURN (ROR)

Rate of return could be confusing, especially when dealing with the stock market. Three measurements are used to discuss a return on an investment. They are: 1) expected return, 2) required return, and 3) realized return. They involve an assessment or determination of the amount of risk to an investment since every investment choice has a concomitant amount of risk associated with it. The greater the risk you are willing to assume, the greater the expected return on your investment. To put it another way, the greater return you want from your investment, the greater the risk you would have to assume. Many economic theories try to measure the relationship between risk and return in markets. There is no perfect crystal ball model. In general, when you are young and have plenty of time to recover from a downturn in an investment, you may choose greater risk to achieve a greater rate of return. As you get older and thus have less time to recover from a downturn or you plan to use soon the wealth built up in your investments, a lower rate of return is more desirable to mitigate risk of loss.

Expected return is the return you, as the investor, believe you will receive on the investment given the amount of risk associated with it. It is forward-looking and made at the time an investment decision is being made. The behind-the-scenes economics with this concept is that the price of an investment is based upon a fair market with a balanced amount of risk for a given amount of return for the risk taken.

Required return is the minimum rate of return that would convince you to invest in a type of investment (given its risk). This measurement deals not with the investor's goals but on the condition of the market when looking to invest. If the market indicates lower returns on an investment given the risk involved, the investor will choose not to invest in that type of investment until market forces change for the better.

Realized return is the return an investor actually receives. It involves a retrospective viewpoint. In other words, it includes the income or capital gain on the investment that the investor earned. If markets were efficient—in other words, if risk and return were in balance—the expected return and required return would be the same. Throughout this book, "rate of return" will mean a realized return.

It is important to understand the concept of risk as it applies to investments. Risk is the tricky part of investing, and it is complicated. Total risk is composed of risk that we cannot control, which is called systematic risk, and risk that we could minimize through proper diversification of our investments, which is called unsystematic risk. No matter how much you diversify your investment portfolio, you cannot minimize systematic risk. Systematic risk involves national and international economic factors: For bonds, this risk involves changes in interest rates, purchasing power (if future inflation decreases the realized gain on an investment), and reinvestment rates (risk that falling interest rates may limit future options for reinvestment). Other systematic risk is inflation, changes in exchange rates, and of course, market risk. Systematic risk you just cannot control or minimize. For securities, this type of risk is associated with the mathematic symbol beta (ß).

With unsystematic risk, a good financial planner can minimize this risk through a proper diversification of investments in a carefully chosen portfolio. Three main types of unsystematic risk exist, all essentially behind the scenes for average investors. It takes much time, knowledge, and understanding of these risks to develop a well-constructed, balanced investment portfolio. For anyone except the very sophisticated investor, this type of knowledge is beyond full comprehension, hence the need for a good financial planner backed by an even stronger money manager.

The first type of unsystematic risk is that associated with a company's type of business (business risk). For instance, utility companies have different risks than healthcare companies, which have different risks than energy companies. The second type of unsystematic risk involves how much debt a company assumes to fuel or finance its operations (financial risk). In simple terms, generally the more debt assumed, the greater the financial risk for that company. The third general unsystematic risk is called political risk and involves the political stability within the country where the company whose stock you seek to invest operates. U.S. companies are generally quite stable, but investment opportunities exist in developing countries or newer markets such as in Russia, China, and Brazil. These nations are less stable politically and have markets that are not as regulated as more developed countries like the United States. In other words, the degree of certainty of the fairness in the stock markets in these countries is not as high as those in the United States and other more mature markets. As a result, the investor cannot assume the markets in these regions are as efficient—fair—as those in the more developed countries.

A good financial planner will first assess your risk tolerance, your budget—income available to invest and debt/expense obligations—along with a myriad of other factors such as future obligations like college tuition payments for children, health concerns, and the investor's age. For example, an investor who in 5-9 years expects to pay tuition payments for children would invest differently than the investor who has toddlers and has much more time before the huge outlay of college tuition or retirement occurs.

Likewise, a senior may have more net income to invest as debt and expense obligations are minimal, but the need for income in retirement and later years is that much sooner than for younger investors. The older investor may require less risky investments, thus an assumption of lower rates of return. The younger investor has more time to recover from a downturn in the market; the older investor does not. (See "Knowing the Time-Value of Money" below for a greater understanding.)

UNDERSTANDING OPPORTUNITY COST

Opportunity cost is an economic concept that refers to, once a decision is made, the loss of potential benefit or gain from the next best choice you could have made but did not choose. In other words, it is what you give up once you make a decision. For instance, if you believed interest rates might increase in the near future and chose to invest in a 3 percent, six-month CD instead of a 4 percent one-year CD, and interest rates declined, the 1 percent in lost interest would be your opportunity cost from choosing to invest in the 3 percent CD instead of the 4 percent one-year CD. Opportunity cost paralyzes some people from making investment decisions for fear of missing out on the "next best choice."

KNOWING THE TIME-VALUE OF MONEY

Time-value of money involves the concept of interest, particularly compounding interest, on periodic investments. To understand the concept, let us first start with taking money you earn and "putting it under the mattress." Consider the impact of inflation on this money. Over time, the money not only will not grow, but it will seem to decrease in value due to inflation. Inflation is when the cost of a certain bundle of goods and services increases over time, thus decreasing the purchasing power or value of the same unit of money/currency it originally possessed. The bundle of goods and services used to measure inflation is the Price Index, which is the average price of a sample of essential U.S. goods and services over a duration of time. An example of the effect of inflation is if you had $100 in the year 2000 to buy certain food items; given the average inflation rate of 2.03 percent from year 2000 to 2020, it would cost $150.22 to purchase the same food items in the year 2020 due to inflation over that twenty-year period. (Pre-COVID, the U.S. Federal Reserve sought to keep the level of inflation at 2.0 percent. It has been much lower than that level, and the Federal Reserve stated at the end of year 2020 that it does not intend to focus on it until the year 2023.) To put this another way, the year 2020 prices are 50.22 percent higher than twenty years ago in the year 2000. Therefore, over time, uninvested wealth—held in the proverbial mattress—is able to buy fewer items due to the increase in the cost of goods and services. Consider the present cost of healthcare; then determine the duration of time until you retire. How much more money would you need to cover healthcare costs then, when you likely will be on a fixed income? How then do you keep up with the rate of inflation?

Now, let us consider the concepts of interest and inflation. Simple interest involves a fixed percentage of return on a principal amount. The formula to calculate simple interest is principal (P) times the annual interest rate (r) times the term (n). It is expressed as:

$$P \times r \times n$$

As an example, assume you invest $100 (P) at an annual interest rate of 5 percent (r) for just one year (n). Your $100 today will be worth $105 in a year ($100 x 5 percent x 1 = $5) because of interest earned over one year. Now, assume you invested the same $100 for five years at 5 percent simple annual interest. Remember, the interest rate is fixed. The formula is: $100 x 5 percent x 5 = $25 in interest earned over five years. Over a thirty-year period the (simple) interest earned would be $150.

Another example of simple interest on an investment is when you invest in a bond, which has attached to it a set amount of interest when you purchase it. You would purchase it for less than its full value or maturity amount. After the time for the bond to mature, it would be worth its face value. For example, a $1,000 bond (maturity value) with a 5 percent coupon (interest) rate might be purchased for $952.38 today. Upon the expiration of the term attached to the bond, it may be cashed in or redeemed for its full $1,000 maturity value. These are examples of simple interest.

Now, let us introduce the concept of compound interest in investing. Compound interest accrues over time and is added back into principal at the end of each term. Then interest accrues during the next term upon the combined principal and previously accumulated interest. In other words, with compounding interest, one earns interest on the interest earned as well as upon the principal. The formula to calculate compound interest is as follows where P is principal, r is the annual interest rate, and n is the term or number of years of investing. Its formula is:

$$P \times (1 + r)^n - P$$

To help explain the concept, consider the following examples.

Example One. Assume you make a one-time investment of $100 at an annual *compound* interest rate of 5 percent, and you do not cash in the investment for thirty years. Instead of the above example on simple interest, at the *end* of every year, the 5 percent return is added back into the principal (the $100 in the first year) and the 5 percent interest rate is applied to that new principal amount over the investment term. The start of year one, the principal or investment amount is $100; at the end of the year (start of year two), the principal amount is $105; at the end of year two, the value is $110.25; at the end of year three, it is $115.76, etc. At the end of a thirty-year period of continuous compounding, with no additional principal added, the investment would yield interest of $432.19.

Example Two. Now let us add a constant *yearly* investment at the *beginning* of each year of $100 starting with the $100 initial investment and 5 percent interest rate over a period of thirty years. The thirty-year return would be $7,408. For a forty-year period, it would be $13,388.

Example Three. Now let us consider continuous *monthly* investments of $100, starting with the same initial $100 investment, 5 percent annual interest rate (annual compounding) for a thirty- and a forty-year period. Over thirty years, the return would be $82,302; over forty years, it would be $149,590.

Example Four. Same parameters, only the investment is $100 each *week* with annual compounding. The thirty-year return is $354,315; forty-year return is $644,137.

As you can see, compounding may occur at different terms—monthly, quarterly, yearly—and it may occur at the end of a certain term or the beginning. The type or frequency of the compounding has a dramatic effect upon the outcome.

The point of this section not only is to show the effect of inflation over time but also the effect of compound interest in investing. A little investment knowledge and discipline early on in life applied over time can make a big difference in your retirement and standard of care in the later years of your life. If a twenty-two-year-old who receives her first job can manage her budget to invest just a small sum consistently over her whole life, the result is dramatic. In Example Three, over forty years, that investor would have enough funds to provide about a year or two of home LTC, depending on the type of care needed and region of the country she lives in. If Example Four applies, the forty-year return would provide about 6-7 years of home LTC services, a dramatic increase in care. More importantly, it gives the investor the economic power to be able to choose to purchase LTC insurance, or to self-pay for LTC needs. See Chapter Four for LTC costs by region.

UNDERSTANDING THE EXTENT OF FDIC PROTECTION ON ACCOUNTS

The Federal Insurance Corporation (FDIC) was created

during the Great Depression by the U.S. Government to provide insurance for bank deposits, thus providing protection to bank depositors and a calming effect to U.S. banking consumers. The initial insurance limit was $2,500 per owner. After many increases over time, as of 2011 with the Dodd-Frank Wall Street Reform and Consumer Protection Act, the insurance limit now is $250,000 per owner. The FDIC reserve is not funded by public funds but primarily by insurance dues of member banks. The key is that each ownership category in each bank is insured. Ownership accounts include retirement accounts, joint accounts, revocable trust accounts, irrevocable trust accounts, employee benefit plan accounts, government accounts, and other single accounts. Each such account is covered by the $250,000 amount. Note that non-qualified investments are not included in this list of covered accounts.

PREPARATION QUESTIONS

1. What are your budget categories? How might you change your priorities to increase your investments and End-Stage security?

2. According to the wealth (net worth) formula, what is your present expected net worth? Are you on target? What obstacles are preventing you from achieving this net worth figure? What are you willing to change in your budget to achieve your desired net worth?

3. How much do you have set aside for an emergency fund? Is that amount adequate in case of an emergency? What changes should you make to how much you allocate to this budget item?

4. What are your debt ratios for your mortgage and non-mortgage debts? Are they within the healthy ratios provided in this chapter? If not, what will you do to operate within healthier debt ratios?

5. Do you require any life insurance given your stage of life, and if so, how much do you require?

6. What action steps do you need to take to investigate long-term care insurance?

7. What qualified and non-qualified investments do you have, and what are your investment balances for each investment?

8. What is the difference between simple interest and compound interest? Do you know how the interest on your investments is calculated?

CHAPTER THREE:

LEARNING ESTATE PLANNING, PROBATE, AND ASSET PROTECTION

"Being prepared is half the victory."

— Miguel De Cervantes

After discussing in the last chapter key concepts of how to build wealth, this chapter discusses how to hold and protect such wealth for yourself and your family. It thus reviews estate planning and asset protection considerations, the probate process, and estate/gift taxes.

UNDERSTANDING ESTATE PLANNING

Proper estate planning goes beyond simply creating a will. Unfortunately, many people, including some lawyers, think that a will suffices for estate planning. Some lawyers choose to pursue additional specialized education after their law degree (called a Juris Doctor or J.D. degree). This next law degree is called a Master of Laws (LL.M. degree). Predominantly LL.M. degrees are in insurance, taxation, or estate planning and elder law, which also involve much education on taxation. In addition, some lawyers who specialize in elder law, an offshoot of the traditional estate planning practice, might be members of The National Academy of Elder Law Attorneys (NAELA). Choosing a lawyer with an LL.M. degree in estate planning/elder law and perhaps who is a member of NAELA may enhance your chance of hiring a lawyer properly knowledgeable in estate planning and elder law matters. Years of experience focused on an estate planning and elder law practice also enhance such chances. Nonetheless, when being represented by a good estate planning attorney, expect the lawyer to do the following:

- Review the types of assets you own and how they are titled.
- Retitle assets so they pass to the intended recipients in the right amount and at such time when the recipient can responsibly manage them, often with an objective of avoiding the probate process.
- Determine if you have any potential estate tax liability and, if so, make suggestions on how to minimize (or eliminate) it.
- Review and provide advice on the liquidity of your estate, especially for long-term care needs, estate taxes, or needs of

a surviving spouse/heir.

- Devise the best asset protection plan given your objectives.
- Review issues of incapacity, long-term care, and/or Medicaid needs and how you may pay for such services.
- Discuss long-term care insurance.
- Discuss, devise, and implement options to provide for heirs with special needs (SN).
- Discuss choosing between a private or public estate plan—a will or trust-based plan.
- Discuss, advise, and implement ways to avoid the probate process.
- Review life insurance needs.
- Discuss issues surrounding the continuation of a closely held business, including rental real estate, in case of an owner's incapacity and death, and develop a business succession plan.
- Review and change beneficiary designations for qualified retirement accounts.
- Assess special issues, such as children born of prior relationships, non-citizenship, unmarried partners, foreign assets, real estate owned outside of one's state of residence, etc.
- Work with your other advisers, such as financial planners and accountants, as needed.

A good estate planning attorney, therefore, should conduct a thorough review of your assets, their values, how they are titled, and how they will transfer upon your death in order to create a proper estate plan for you. (See Exhibits D-F of this book for a sample attorney intake.) Furthermore, at various stages of your life, your estate planning objectives may change, necessitating further review and revision. A simple estate plan may involve a will, a medical directive or healthcare power (also called proxies and directives, depending upon the state), and a financial power (called a power of attorney). In certain stages of your life, depending on the type of assets you own and to whom you wish to transfer them, perhaps a will is not necessary. In other cases, a revocable (also called inter-vivos) trust is appropriate.

AVOIDING THE PROBATE PROCESS

The probate administration of a decedent's estate is a government process that enables the decedent's creditors to collect upon that person's outstanding debts at death and to ensure the proper transfer of the decedent's assets to his or her heirs or chosen beneficiaries. For a person dying without a will, states have a statutory one-size-fits-all delineation for beneficiaries of probate assets. This type of probate estate is called an intestate estate. In many cases, however, this intestacy statute may be insufficient to accomplish your desires and objectives. To better understand the probate process and how assets in general transfer upon death, it is important first to understand which assets are probate assets, and which assets are non-probate assets.

The following graphic shows general types of asset classes that one may own upon death. Gross Taxable Estate (GTE) includes all assets owned by a decedent or that the decedent has some type of beneficial interest and control over according to the IRS Code.

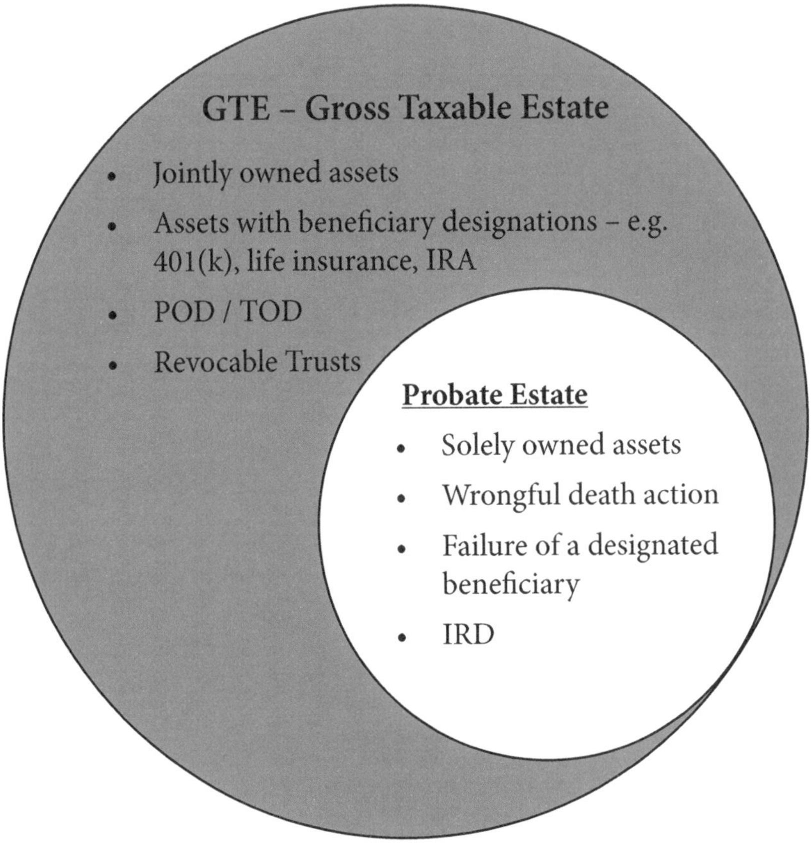

Difference between Gross Estate and Probate Estate

Note that the list of probate assets, which might look slightly different in some states, is a smaller subset of this GTE category. An example of how states treat assets differently would be a wrongful death action claim. Such a claim results when someone has killed someone else; e.g., a gas truck driver driving recklessly hit and killed the decedent. In California, a wrongful death action claim is brought by the surviving spouse/family, and thus not a probate asset, whereas in many other states, it would be an action by the executor of the decedent's estate, and thus, an estate asset. The main point is that solely owned assets pass through the probate process since no other designation or legal determination exists to control their successor ownership. Likewise, income earned before your death, yet received after death, also is considered a probate asset. This income under the IRC is called income in respect of a decedent, or IRD. Your will only directs how probate assets are transferred; it has no control over the direction of other non-probate assets. Therefore, to create an efficient estate plan, the lawyer first must understand how your assets are titled and will transfer upon death given such ownership. The takeaway is that once you understand how your estate assets are titled and thus transfer upon death, with your lawyer's guidance, you can carefully start to create an estate plan that may involve retitling them to avoid the probate process, which is generally undesired because it is public in nature, timely, and involves extra costs and fees. Most people believe that a will manages every asset they own when they die, but with careful planning, your eventual plan may result in your will controlling an exceedingly small (or zero) percentage of your entire estate. In addition, understanding and re-titling assets accordingly is not a costly process, yet it may reduce much cost, and aggravation, for your loved ones later by avoiding the probate process.

An example of assets that pass outside of the probate process is jointly held assets in which ownership simply passes to the other surviving owner(s) upon one owner's death. There are, however, some jointly held assets that are not treated as held in survivorship. These assets, instead, are held as "tenants-in-common." The decedent's ownership interest in an asset titled in this manner would not automatically pass to the survivor owners but would be treated as a solely owned interest, and thus controlled by the probate process. For this reason, it is important to look at the root document that creates your jointly owned property interest. Another example of a non-probate asset is property held in a trust. Trust property is controlled by the trust's terms and provisions, and its assets pass pursuant to its terms, not by the terms of a will. Investments with beneficiary designations, such as qualified retirement accounts and life insurance policies, also are not probate assets because they transfer to the asset's living designated beneficiaries. However, if the designated appointment fails—for instance, no designated beneficiary is then living—the asset defaults to the decedent's probate estate, and its disposition then is controlled by the will. Lastly, some bank accounts may have Transfer-on-Death (TOD) or Payable-on-Death (POD) designations that enable the account assets to bypass the probate process and pass outright to the designated individual(s). Thus, through a careful review of your estate, and depending upon your objectives, types of assets, and how they are titled, a good estate planner could create an efficient plan that avoids the probate process. In addition, if you own real property in a state other than the one in which you live, it may entail another ancillary probate administration where the real property is located. With proper attention to detail, an ancillary probate administration also can be avoided.

Another goal besides avoiding probate is protecting assets for both the client and his or her ultimate beneficiaries. Toward this goal, the lawyer also must determine how to shield a client from issues like lawsuits, potential estate taxes, and an heir or beneficiary who might be a spendthrift or engage in negative behaviors such as abusing drugs or engaging in cult or other such activities. Another goal may be to protect a beneficiary with special needs through properly sheltering assets. Depending upon the situation, the lawyer also may conduct a Medicaid spend-down analysis. Furthermore, besides knowing how to draft a will or other estate planning documents, a good estate planning lawyer should be knowledgeable with prenuptial agreements, real estate law, family (divorce) law, closely-held business issues, asset protection (creditor rights), and Medicaid rules, in addition to probate rules, governing statutes, and estate, gift, and other taxes.

LEARNING ABOUT ESTATE AND GIFT TAXES

Estate planning lawyers manipulate three main tax considerations: the estate tax exemption, the annual gift tax exclusion, and the marital deduction. The first two exempt and exclude wealth from taxes; the third defers estate taxes for a surviving spouse. The fiduciary of a decedent's estate must report all of the decedent's GTE on a federal estate tax form if the value of his or her assets surpasses a certain amount. This amount is called the estate tax exemption. The federal estate tax exemption increased to $11.58 million in the year 2020, and barring a change in the tax law, it will be adjusted upward for inflation until the year 2026, at which time it reverts back to a base $5 million exemption (as of year 2011). Likewise, if the existing tax law is repealed prior to year 2025, the exemption amount will revert to this base $5 million. This new exemption amount, in turn, will be adjusted for inflation from the year 2010 forward, creating a 2026 federal exemption amount of $6.59 million.

If a decedent's estate is valued below the applicable exemption in the year of death, a federal estate tax form does not need to be filed for federal estate tax purposes. However, you may file it for other reasons, mainly to preserve any unused exemption amount above the decedent's GTE value for the benefit of the decedent's surviving spouse's estate upon his or her subsequent death. This transfer process of the unused exemption is generically called portability.[8] Beware, though; some states also impose their own stand-alone state estate or inheritance tax with its own corresponding exemption amount. The unused state exemption amount does not have a portability feature, creating added complexity to estate planning in such states, especially in a state like Massachusetts, which only has a $1 million state estate tax exemption.[9]

Gift and federal estate taxes are connected. First, a U.S. citizen may gift up to a certain amount called the annual gift tax exclusion, which, too, is adjusted for inflation yearly and rounded to the nearest $1,000. In year 2020, this exclusion amount is $15,000 per year, per person (donee). Any gifting above this threshold is considered a taxable gift and must be reported on a gift tax return and filed the April following the year of the gift. It is taxable because you may gift during your lifetime up to the estate tax exemption before being required to pay a federal gift tax. Then, upon death, there is an adjustment to the federal estate tax exemption by subtracting from it all taxable gifts made during your lifetime. For this reason, the gift and estate tax exemptions are called unified. For Connecticut residents, the state imposes a state gift tax in the same manner. As of July 1, 2013, Minnesota joined Connecticut as the only states with their own gift tax.

Presently, the federal estate tax is a flat 40 percent tax on any taxable assets. States with their own estate tax generally have increasing marginal estate tax rates that generally cap at 16 percent. This state estate tax is in addition to the federal estate tax, although the federal government allows a credit for the state estate taxes paid. It is important to note that gifting and estate planning issues change for resident, non-U.S. spouses, and for non-resident individuals owning property in the United States. In addition, those states without a stand-alone estate tax share a small portion of the federal estate tax. This "shared" tax is generically called a "sponge" tax.

KNOWING WILLS

A will is the instructions of the testator (the person making the will) as to whom he or she wants probate assets to pass (technically called legatees, and for real property, devisees; generically called beneficiaries) after payment of funeral/burial expenses, creditors, taxes, administrative (probate, legal, accounting, appraisal, etc.) costs, and fees. During the probate administration process, the appointed executor (or administrator) holds title to the decedent's assets in a fiduciary capacity and manages them under court supervision. At the end of a probate administration period, the probate court orders the outright transfer of all remaining probate assets to the testator's beneficiaries. A will, unlike a trust, does not direct the fiduciary to hold assets for a beneficiary's benefit, as you might wish to do for various reasons, but commonly for tax avoidance, or to protect a surviving spouse or younger beneficiaries who are deemed unable to manage properly an inheritance or who legally may not. (See the section on trusts below regarding this scenario.) Many issues exist with how assets transfer to intended beneficiaries with wills. Three main issues with interpreting wills are: 1) how the underlying assets are categorized, 2) how the clause that makes the gift in the will is drafted, and 3) the use of statutory laws that affect gifting clauses.

The first important issue to understand with wills is how assets are legally categorized to know how they are treated in the probate administration process. One category of assets gifted in a will is of tangible personal property, which are the things you physically own, such as your clothes, furniture, jewelry, automobile, etc. Another category is of intangible assets you own an interest in, but the status of the assets is not physical like tangible ones. Examples of intangible assets are stocks, contract rights, business interests, royalties, etc. A third general category is real estate that is called real property under the law.

The second issue involves the proper use of gifting terms and how the lawyer drafts a gifting clause. The more precise the will drafting is, the more likely the estate will avoid undesired consequences, such as lawsuits on interpretation, income tax consequences, an unintended disinheritance, or a greater transfer of assets to a beneficiary or beneficiaries than the testator desired. A good estate planner not only will anticipate and advise for such issues but also adroitly draft the will accordingly. How such assets are gifted in the will may impact the management of the estate and who gets what. For instance, what if an estate asset receives income during the administration period? Who should receive that income, during the administration process—the estate for general use, or the person gifted the income-producing asset in the will? The answer depends on how the lawyer drafted the gifting clause of the underlying asset in the will.

One way to draft a gift in a will is by a specific clause, such as: "I give and bequeath $1,000 from my Bank of America savings account ending in x1234 to my brother Robert." Another way is via a general clause, such as: "I give and bequeath $1,000 to my brother Robert." Assets also may be gifted via a residuary clause, such as: "All of the rest, residue and remainder of my assets, I give, bequeath, and devise to my brother Robert." In each case, who gets the income earned from the account during the administration period? For a specific gift, Robert. Maybe not for the general gift since a specific asset was not listed to pay the $1,000 gift. As part of the residuary gift, the income passes to the estate for general use. It is important, therefore, to discuss your gifting intentions with your lawyer so the will may be drafted appropriately.

The last typical category for gifting is called the residuary or residual share, which includes all remaining probate assets not already gifted in the will by previous provisions. Various ways exist to draft the disposition of the remaining assets, and if a lawyer does not draft with the necessary particularity, unintended consequences may ensue. Although you could list specific shares or percentages to a list of successor beneficiaries in your will, often gifts for residuary gifts might say: "to my spouse, if living, and if not living, to my children, *per stirpes*." Lawyers use a drafting technique when making class gifts—gifts to a group of people such as to children or siblings—by using two Latin phrases that assist with avoiding a long-drafted paragraph to handle a distribution clause. The phrases are *per stirpes* and *per capita. Per stirpes* means "by representation"; in other words, if a beneficiary dies, his or her share shall pass equally to his or her children, and, in turn, if a child in this next hereditary line has died leaving living children, equally to that deceased child's children, and so on. If the deceased beneficiary has no living descendants, then that gift ends and becomes part of the assets gifted to the remaining class members of the same hereditary class of the deceased beneficiary. *Per capita* means the opposite, only the living members of the class take a share in the gift—class survivors take, not descendants of a deceased class member.

One unintended consequence involves the lack of foresight when using a particular gifting clause. For instance, what if there are too few assets to cover the administrative expenses and all gifts made in the will? Which gifts to beneficiaries should be reduced or voided? Does it matter? Knowing how you desire assets to be managed dictates how the gifting clauses in the will should be drafted. If, for some reason, the estate value at death is less than its value when you executed your will, such that the full amount of all gifts may not be satisfied, the key is knowing which dispositions are least and most protected. Specifically gifted assets have the highest priority of protection from invasion; gifts made via a residuary clause have the least priority of protection, although if assets pass via intestacy, those assets are invaded before residuary assets. Why is this important? Because given how the clauses are drafted in the will, specific gifts or amounts to ancillary beneficiaries may have higher protection from invasion than those to your primary beneficiaries, like children if the gifts to the primary beneficiaries are made via a residuary clause. The specific gifts then may be untouched, while the children will receive a smaller percentage of the estate than you might have intended. Therefore, if a will is not drafted carefully, the testator's objectives may be unintendedly thwarted. Too many lawyers do not consider this issue when drafting.

To demonstrate the third issue with interpreting will clauses, what happens if the named beneficiary in your will dies before you do? Who then would receive the deceased beneficiary's share—that beneficiary's children or would that gift end (lapse)? And, if it ends, what part of the will would control the distribution of that lapsed gift? Assuming we are not dealing with a class gift in which *per stirpes* or *per capita* would control, if the will clearly states an alternate beneficiary, given such occurrence, that alternate beneficiary should receive the gift. However, in the absence of a clear alternate taker, some states have statutes called anti-lapse statutes that force takers of lapsed gifts, which makes it not only important for the drafting lawyer to carefully understand your intentions but also to know how such statutes may control and unwittingly change your gifting intentions. In some cases, the drafting lawyer specifically will make this anti-lapse statute inapplicable for the administration of the will, especially in a few such states that disregard commonly drafted phrases, such as "if living" or "if the beneficiary has survived," when there is no further direction for an alternate beneficiary. Such states do not assume that a gift with such language simply lapses. Instead, the anti-lapse clause may be applied and the deceased beneficiary's descendants receive the gift according to the anti-lapse statute. Without your clearly communicating your intentions and the lawyer's particular drafting, your probate assets may pass to unintended beneficiaries or in unintended amounts.

Again, consider how you want a gift to transfer if a named beneficiary has died. If the will instructs the personal representative (or executor) to provide percentages to a list of beneficiaries, and one of those beneficiaries has died with no stated alternate beneficiary, that share might lapse and pass via your state's intestacy or anti-lapse statute. Thus, a careful drafter must consider how to handle a potential lapse with appropriate distribution provisions.

KNOWING TRUSTS

For trusts, unlike wills, a trustee is the fiduciary (versus an executor or personal representative when in probate court) who holds, manages, and distributes trust assets (its corpus) for the stated purposes in the trust document. The trust may instruct the trustee to distribute income and/or principal to a beneficiary, typically for health, education, or living expenses. The trust may also instruct the trustee to distribute a percentage of trust income to a beneficiary. In addition, upon triggering events stated in the trust, income and/or principal from a beneficiary's trust share could be withdrawn by a beneficiary. Triggering events listed in the trust may be when a spouse dies, a child attains a certain age, or when a beneficiary dies. Another triggering event may involve the grant of a withdrawal right when a beneficiary attains a certain age or ages.

Typical reasons for using trusts are:

- To avoid the public nature of the probate process.
- To handle a quicker, smoother transition in the management of assets upon a maker's (grantor's or settlor's) disability, which may avoid a guardianship or conservatorship action in probate court, or death.
- To allow the use of a home for a beneficiary's life or a term, particularly for a second spouse, thereby preserving the home for children of a prior relationship upon the surviving spouse's death (or the established term).
- To shelter assets for estate tax purposes in order to double the available estate tax exemption[10] for each spouse.
- To manage assets for beneficiaries who do not manage wealth well.
- To avoid assets passing to a son-in-law or daughter-in-law instead of a child's descendants (the biological grandchildren).
- To shelter assets from a beneficiary's creditors.

- To provide for a beneficiary with special needs.
- To transfer assets out of the grantor's taxable estate to avoid estate taxes.

While the grantor is alive, in many instances, he or she is the trustee who manages the trust corpus. Successor trustees are appointed in the case of disability, death, or resignation of a prior named trustee. The trustee manages the trust assets according to the trust's terms and provisions, which are carefully constructed by the drafting lawyer and client. Although many types of trusts exist, two general trust types are: 1) revocable (also called inter-vivos trusts), which the grantor may amend or alter at any time he or she is competent; and 2) irrevocable, which the grantor generally may not modify, alter, or amend.[11] Revocable trusts are considered "pass through" trusts in that the tax identification number for them is the grantor's Social Security number and all items of income and expense are reported on the grantor's income tax return. Transferring assets into and out of the trust, therefore, does not create a gift or income taxable event. There are many types of irrevocable trusts, which are more complicated to draft given the many tax aspects involved. Many irrevocable trusts are taxable entities as opposed to the pass-through treatment of revocable (technically grantor) trusts. For these trusts, the grantor (or trustee) must obtain a new tax identification (or employer identification number—EIN), and depending upon the trust activity, a separate trust income tax must be reported yearly (on a 1041 form). Income accrued from assets held in such irrevocable trusts is taxed at the highest marginal income tax rate; however, the trustee could make this income distributable to trust beneficiaries (reported on a K1 form and issued to beneficiaries), who likely have lower marginal income tax rates. Such income is then reported on the beneficiary's income tax return.

Another benefit of revocable trusts is the use of the marital deduction when the first spouse dies. If the first spouse dies with a GTE greater than the applicable estate tax exemption, a trust drafted to efficiently handle this purpose typically bifurcates into a tax-exempt sub-trust and a tax-deferred sub-trust. The assets held in the exempt trust, and their growth, are exempt from estate taxes. However, with a properly drafted trust, instead of the imposition of an estate tax on any amount greater than the estate tax exemption, the trust holds such assets for the benefit of a surviving spouse deferring the estate tax that otherwise would be due. The marital deduction may also apply to a decedent's non-trust assets valued over the estate tax exemption that passes to the surviving spouse. The value of any assets held in the marital deduction sub-trust, or otherwise deferred by use of the marital deduction, are taxed for estate tax purposes upon the surviving spouse's death. The deferred assets escape this eventual estate tax to the extent of their exhaustion upon the surviving spouse's death below his or her applicable estate tax exemption amount.

Lastly, the trust duration depends upon the specific terms of the trust and the laws of the jurisdiction (the state) that apply to that trust. For instance, the terms of a trust may state that upon the youngest child of the grantor becoming age thirty-five, all trust assets must pass outright to the trust beneficiaries. Or a trust by its terms may keep assets in trust for the benefit of its beneficiaries for as long as applicable law allows. States typically establish by statute the longest term in which the trust may last before it must terminate, which may be a certain number of years once the trust becomes irrevocable, such as 90 or 800 years, or a measurement of the lives of certain beneficiaries (pursuant to a common law or statutory Rule against Perpetuities). Other states allow for trusts to continue in perpetuity, often with robust asset protection laws that protect against a creditor's attachment of trust property. (See Chapter Twelve.) Unlike with wills, there is no discernable gap in the ownership of trust assets. If the grantor of the trust were a trustee upon death, the next named trustee assumes the role as successor trustee. There is no delay for the appointment of a fiduciary as there is in probate court with a will.

As an example of the ease with using trusts, consider a husband and wife who are having a family reunion in San Francisco, California. They notice the *entire* family is there—all of their appointed executors, trustees, healthcare agents, and attorneys-in-fact—and the next day, together they are *all* flying to Hawaii. Frantically, the couple calls their lawyer about what to do. The lawyer asks if the hotel has email so he may email them newly drafted updated documents that both clients can print out and sign before they leave for Hawaii. Within an hour or so, a trust amendment, codicil, medical directive, and power of attorney with new appointees for each is emailed to the hotel. The next morning, a copy of the newly executed estate planning documents is scanned and emailed back to the lawyer's office. Problem solved.

In another trust issue scenario, a client calls his attorney from his convertible while entering the highway to come home after a weekend with his family down south. He emphatically explains that he just left his family get-together and must quickly delete the gift to his nephew as a beneficiary of his trust, all quarter of a million dollars of it. The next day, the client has an amendment to his trust in his email box to execute at his local bank, which he did that day! Will that nephew ever learn that whatever he did or said that weekend cost him a nice inheritance?

Once you have chosen to use a trust as a component of your estate plan, how do you choose who should be the successor trustee after you? There are three key considerations for the selection of a successor trustee. The first consideration involves the trustee's duties and responsibilities and whether the prospective trustee has the requisite knowledge, skill, and time to carry out such duties. The second consideration is the prospective trustee's disposition in successfully working with beneficiaries. The third consideration is your level of trust in the prospective trustee to manage the trust funds for the benefit of your chosen beneficiaries according to your expressed desires.

Among the primary duties and responsibilities of a trustee is the responsibility to choose appropriate investments given the trust's purpose. The trustee should, therefore, be competent and prudent with this endeavor. He or she should understand income and estate tax matters, since managing trust assets (perhaps of many different asset classes) is a key responsibility that entails many tax decisions and consequences. Some trusts provide the trustee discretion to convert a beneficiary's separate trust share into a special (or supplemental) needs trust if a beneficiary is disabled and able to benefit from public assistance programs. So, knowledge of, or time and ability to learn, Medicaid and other state programs also may be important. Additionally, knowledge of trust and estate law is helpful to handle complicated issues such as the: 1) timing of distributions; 2) determination of which assets to sell based on their cost basis for the purposes of making trust distributions, expense payments, and tax payments, without unnecessarily incurring more tax consequences; 3) legal interpretation of the distribution terms and conditions of the trust; and 4) investment requirements necessary to balance the needs of the present income beneficiaries with those of the remainder beneficiaries.

Below is a list of typical trustee duties and responsibilities from the legal perspective.

- Take possession of the trust property, keep it in the trustee's custody as a fiduciary and manage it in accordance with the trust terms.
- Comply with orders of the court, if any, that control the trust estate.
- Safeguard, preserve, and protect the trust property against loss, dissipation, or diminution, and likewise, execute any proper contracts, incur debts, and make expenditures as are necessary and proper, including prosecuting and defending any suits and court proceedings to protect the trust property.
- Insure the trust estate.
- Make improvements to trust property as authorized by the trust.
- Perform the trust administration loyally and faithfully.
- Not delegate trustee duties to another, other than purely ministerial powers.
- Not exercise self-dealing; at all times, the trustee

must act in the beneficiaries' interests according to the trust terms.

- Not privately use, apply, or appropriate trust property, unless with express consent of all beneficiaries.
- Maintain the prudent person standard (how a person of prudence, discretion, and intelligence would manage his or her own financial affairs), and exercise due care and skill while acting as trustee.
- Be fair in any dealings with a beneficiary.
- If a business is part of the trust property, conduct the business as required by the trust and according to its grantor's intentions.
- Not commit waste—the trustee must make the trust principal productive.
- Not conduct risky investments, but rather, follow the prudent investment rule (a legal doctrine that requires a fiduciary to prudently assess risk and return when investing). Thus, the trustee must exercise the care, diligence, and skill of an ordinary prudent person in making, retaining, disposing, or changing trust investments. Advice of a financial planner is preferable.
- Not commingle trust funds with the trustee's own

funds; keep trust funds in a reputable banking/investment institution and titled appropriately as trust assets.

- Distribute trust property appropriately to the beneficiaries according to the trust terms.
- Keep accurate records and file all required income tax returns. Working with an accountant is preferable.
- Keep and render to beneficiaries a full and accurate record and accounting of the trust assets and investments according to the trust terms or court decree.
- Seek appropriate professional advice—legal, accounting, financial, realtors, appraisals, etc.—as is appropriate to adhere to the trustee duties at all times.

In addition to possessing the requisite knowledge and skill to manage trust assets, the trustee also must have a suitable disposition to competently serve in this role. In working with the trust beneficiaries, a trustee must be capable of navigating factors such as age, maturity, health issues, marital influences, and risky lifestyle choices. Sometimes the trustee's job involves identifying a beneficiary's harmful behavior and managing the distributions of trust funds in a way that does not condone or support such behavior. The trustee, therefore, may face difficult decisions and must have the fortitude and compassion to act properly.

Lastly, consider the length of time the trust may exist and

your confidence in an appointed successor trustee to manage the trust funds in the future. Appointing a trustee and successor trustees is a task not to be taken lightly. For this reason, some people choose institutional trustees such as banks or trust companies; others choose accountants or estate planning attorneys. Trustees are entitled to a fair and reasonable fee. Institutional trustees publish rates for their charges. Cost, therefore, is a consideration, but so, too, is the proper management of the trust for the benefit of your loved ones—the beneficiaries of your trust.

UNDERSTANDING MEDICAL DIRECTIVES

A medical directive, also called an advance healthcare directive or healthcare proxy, appoints an agent (and successors) to make medical decisions for the maker—called the principal—in case the principal is unable to do so him- or herself. It also may include a living will (which may also be done in a separate document) that states in general terms that in the case of the principal having a debilitating event, not to apply life-support measures to prolong life when in the opinion of a treating physician (and perhaps also a specialist), nothing more can be done to prolong life but for life-support. Each state has slightly different wording to describe this debilitating determination. Statutory terms used are of a terminal condition, permanent unconsciousness, permanent incapacity, or a vegetative state. Massachusetts, in particular, does not statutorily allow one to execute a living will, but the medical profession has its own forms to circumvent such legal omission. The form is called the Massachusetts Medical Orders for Life-Sustaining Treatment or MOLST. The medical directives and living wills go beyond a mere Do Not Resuscitate (DNR) order. Note that assisted death by a non-physician is against the law in any state in the United States. Physician-assisted death, however, is legal in the following states: California, Colorado, District of Columbia, Hawaii, Maine, Montana, New Jersey, Oregon, Vermont, and Washington.

In a medical directive, you may appoint agents to handle health decisions for you when you are unable to do so. The agent also enforces your living will. A conservator (guardian) of your person may also be designated in case one is needed in the future.

USING FINANCIAL POWERS

A financial power is called a (general) power of attorney or durable power of attorney. This type of document involves a principal (maker) appointing agents (or attorneys-in-fact) to have certain powers specified in the document to be performed for the principal. A general power of attorney ceases to have affect upon the incapacity of the principal. A durable power of attorney is drafted so it does not become inoperable upon the principal's subsequent disability. Both a general power of attorney and a durable power of attorney no longer have any effect or power when the principal dies. Many agents under a power of attorney are surprised that upon the principal's death and before a personal representative (executor) is appointed under the will, they no longer have control over the decedent's solely owned assets. (Revisit the above section on trusts on how to avoid this issue.) A power of attorney gives as much or as little authority as the principal desires. Do not take these documents for granted. Carefully review and discuss the powers granted in your power of attorney with your attorney before you sign it because they give powers to your agent over all facets of your financial life.

DISCOVERING ASSET PROTECTION

Various asset protection concerns are handled with estate planning. Examples of concerns giving rise to such asset protection are creditor attachment, divorce, preventing family assets from passing to non-biological heirs, Medicaid eligibility, and providing funds for a special needs (SN) beneficiary without foreclosing options for state benefits. Creating a trust to shelter assets in many states may not be enough to shield assets from the grantor's creditors, a Medicaid application, or special needs matters. Laws that disallow a grantor to shelter assets from his or her creditors by putting assets into a trust apply the concept of the "self-settled" trust rule; thus in those states, your own trust, in which you benefit from the trust, does not shelter assets. However, some states allow various types of sheltering in their jurisdiction with the use of certain irrevocable self-settled trusts. These trusts are called Domestic Asset Protection Trusts (DAPTs). States that allow them are: Alaska, Connecticut, Delaware, Hawaii, Mississippi, Missouri, Nevada, New Hampshire, Ohio, Oklahoma, Rhode Island, South Dakota, Tennessee, Utah, Virginia, West Virginia, and Wyoming. One way to provide some protection upon divorce, even in states that apply the self-settled rule, may be to create a revocable trust prior to marriage and fund the trust with non-marital assets (and not using such assets for marital purposes). This measure is a clear indication to a judge in a marital dissolution (divorce) action that you never intended to commingle such personal or family assets in the trust and that you never intended to make them marital assets subject to division in the dissolution of marriage action. A pre-nuptial agreement would go even further, providing additional clear intent and, thus, more protection.

To preserve assets for a beneficiary with special needs, a lawyer must carefully draft a particular trust that adheres to complicated federal and state-specific requirements. These trusts could be revocable or irrevocable, depending upon circumstances and purpose. In addition, in some cases, the trust must be approved by the state attorney general to ensure the trust is drafted so that its assets are properly set aside for the benefit of the special needs beneficiary and the state upon the beneficiary's death, if state benefits were provided to the beneficiary. For trusts that will hold the special needs beneficiary's property—a self-settled trust—there must be a provision for state repayment upon the death of the SN person for public assistance given to that person throughout his or her life. These trusts are generically called first-party SNTs or (d)(4)(A) trusts because they must conform to 42 U.S.C. §1396(p)(d)(4)(A). They are available for a disabled person under the age of sixty-five. Trusts funded by someone other than the SN person may have provisions to avoid such state repayment. These trusts are complicated, so it is essential to use estate planners knowledgeable with drafting SN trusts.

Some irrevocable trusts, drafted properly, may shelter assets from creditors. However, generally, the greater the sheltering, the greater the loss of control, if any, the grantor will have over the trust assets. For instance, you may create an irrevocable trust and each year gift assets to it that are valued below the annual exclusion amount for the benefit of each trust beneficiary. Since the value of the gifted assets for each beneficiary is below the gift tax threshold, the gifts are not taxable. These beneficiaries could be your children, other family members, friends, etc. For instance, if you named your three living children and two living grandchildren as trust beneficiaries, you may gift to the trust each year any amount up to $15,000 times these five trust beneficiaries up to a total of $75,000 without being subject to a gift tax, or a later reduction in the estate tax exemption upon your death. Your spouse may do the same, depending upon how the trust is drafted. You, and sometimes your spouse, if he or she is a beneficiary, generally will not be a trustee of the trust. Over many years, this type of trust could enable wealthier individuals and couples to transfer assets outside of their gross taxable estate (GTE) to benefit chosen beneficiaries and escape estate taxes through a carefully executed estate plan. However, keep in mind that for this type of trust to be effective, you will neither be the trustee nor may trust assets be distributed back to you from the trust.[12]

Retirement funds in a 401(k) are protected against creditor attachment by private creditors.[13] Other qualified funds, disability, veterans' payments, and Social Security benefits are also protected by federal law from private creditor attachment and are generally protected in bankruptcy proceedings. They also bypass the probate process, assuming a beneficiary is designated and the designated person is then living. Non-qualified assets have no similar federal protection, although states allow certain minimal exemption amounts on such assets.

DEVELOPING YOUR ESTATE PLAN

As will be discussed further in this book, the proper estate plan for you depends upon the stage of your life and your objectives and concerns. It also depends upon the amount of your wealth. When attaining majority age (generally age eighteen), medical directives may be the only estate planning consideration. When buying a home and starting a family, a will, medical directives, and perhaps a power of attorney may suffice to protect yourself, although trusts for minor children may be appropriate. As discussed above, trusts may protect heirs unable to manage wealth, or simply provide more privacy considering inheritance or wealth matters. Without careful preparation for your End-Stage security, in your latter stage of life you may have to undergo a carefully executed Medicaid spend-down plan and revisions to your estate plan. Throughout your life, however, do not plan only for retirement, as the many financial planning commercials remind us, but also plan for your End-Stage security.

More advanced estate planning is needed for prodigious accumulators of wealth to avoid estate taxes and plan a strategic transfer of wealth to family or even charitable entities. With a carefully planned and well-executed strategy, you may transfer sizeable wealth to such beneficiaries without incurring gift or estate taxes. As with building wealth, such a plan requires time to implement. Consult the last chapter of this book for such advanced estate planning ideas. As always, seek an experienced estate planning attorney to create your high net worth estate plan.

PREPAREDNESS QUESTIONS

1. Compile your assets, how they are titled and their values, and determine which assets pass via probate.

2. For all qualified assets and life insurance policies, list your designated beneficiaries. Obtain copies of your beneficiary appointments for your and your estate planning lawyer's records. If you do not have contingent beneficiaries, obtain a change of beneficiary form from the company that handles the investment and appoint successor beneficiaries. Make sure you keep a copy of the new beneficiary appointments for your records.

3. Have you created an estate plan? If yes, review your will to make sure it is drafted in a manner that reflects how you wish your assets to transfer upon death. Pay particular attention to how the gifting clauses are drafted in the will after learning the different types of clauses used to transfer probate assets in this chapter. Does the manner in which the will is drafted protect your primary beneficiaries? Are grandchildren included in the will? (Look for phrases like *per stirpes*.) Is the

will properly drafted to avoid the anti-lapse clause? If you do not have a will, determine if you need one, and after compiling the data from question one, contact an estate planning attorney.

4. Next, review your medical directive and financial power of attorney. Review the people appointed in them, the order in which they are appointed, and consider if those appointments are acceptable or if you wish to change them. Make sure these documents have HIPAA (Health Insurance Portability and Accountability Act) waivers in them. If not, execute new ones.

5. Determine if a will suffices for your estate and estate planning objectives or if a trust better serves you. Contact your estate planning lawyer if you desire a trust to be part of your estate plan.

6. If you have a trust, make the same review of it as question three above for your will. Is the trust drafted as you wish?

Years	Annual Exclusion	Years	Annual Exclusion
1997-2000	$10,000	2009-2012	$13,000
2001-2005	$11,000	2013-2017	$14,000
2006-2008	$12,000	2018-2020	$15,000

7. Determine if you have made any taxable gifts based upon the annual exclusion amounts listed below. Keep such gifts in your estate planning records. Any gifts over the annual exclusion in a year require that you file a gift tax return.

8. Have you chosen the best trustee for your trust, if any?

9. If you have adult children, have they executed a healthcare directive? If not, especially if college students, have them execute one to appoint you.

CHAPTER FOUR:

PREPARING FOR ILLNESS

"It's better to prepare and prevent than to repair and repent."

— Ezra Taft Benson

Many of us will require long-term care (LTC) assistance. Providing care within the family is not only financially costly but emotionally demanding on family caregivers, a majority of whom have been women. Failing to prepare well in advance of, or even to notice signs for, care needs exacerbates this emotional and financial stress of caring for an individual in need. Many people believe Medicare will cover all healthcare costs. This is not so. This chapter examines the statistics on need, the stress on caregivers, and early signs to notice that indicate need. The next chapter will discuss the average costs by region of the United States for various types of LTC coverage, average duration needs for care, and typical planning challenges during various stages of your life, adding estate planning considerations for each stage.

SEEING THE STATISTICS

Many people either ignore future LTC matters or accept them but are ignorant of the financial and emotional costs when a person requires assistance with Activities of Daily Living (ADLs).[14] In this area, people generally are reactive, not proactive. According to the U.S. Department of Health and Human Services, 70 percent of U.S. individuals sixty-five years of age or older will require some type of LTC assistance.[15] Are you prepared? Will your plan burden your loved ones? Will your plan provide you with the best care? What are your options? And since Medicare was never designed to pay for LTC, how will you pay for it?

Some people believe they will not live long enough to worry about LTC. The average life expectancy, men and women combined, in the United States as of 2020 is about seventy-nine years.[16] Women, however, typically live 5-6 years longer than men in the United States, pointing to a greater concern for women regarding long-term care needs in their later years. Since life expectancy figures are averages, 50 percent of us will live longer than these mean ages. Considering longevity in your family, your health habits, and your lifestyle, you may be among the 7 out of 10 people in the United States who will require LTC assistance. Being proactive with preparing for cognitive impairment or declining abilities with ADLs likely will have profound benefits—emotionally and financially—to you and your family caregiver.

For instance, a 2018 Genworth-sponsored study called Beyond Dollars[17] reported of family caregivers:

- 70 percent missed time from work
- 46 percent were forced to work less (20 percent reduced work by ten hours or more a week)
- 9 percent lost their jobs due to caregiving duties
- 50 percent believed their careers were negatively affected
- 30 percent felt they lost career opportunities
- For care recipients who had LTC insurance, family care providers reported less negative emotional strain compared to those who did not have LTC insurance coverage. Stress was 40 percent compared to 52 percent; depression was 25 percent compared to 32 percent; and a sense of isolation was 16 percent compared to 21 percent.

The cost for such care may be devastating. Although prior surveys reported a greater percentage of women bearing caregiver duties—about 60 percent to 40 percent of men—the Beyond Dollars study reported equal caregiving duties between women and men. Besides experiencing lost wages for time off to attend to caregiving duties, sometimes the family caregiver simultaneously is raising or helping his or her children. Members of this group are called the Sandwich Generation. While the emotional and financial stress of these responsibilities puts them at risk, caregivers also experience decreased time for their personal health and security. According to a 2019 study by Home Instead, Inc., a franchisor of the Home Instead Senior Care® network,[18] 63 percent of this Sandwich Generation report their caregiving role makes it more difficult to care for themselves. Fifty-two percent claim it has led to depression, and 45 percent report it has delayed their retirement.

Such caregiving duties may impact women more since they tend to live longer than men and historically tend to be more risk adverse in investing than men. They take less risk with investments; thus, they tend to generate less wealth than men (estimated at about one quarter less). Along with the trauma of outliving a loved one is the fear of outliving savings and investments to meet future needs. Consider that:

- 75 percent of residents in nursing facilities are women.
- Nearly 50 percent of all female nursing facility residents rely on Medicaid for their long-term care services.
- Women are 71 percent more likely than men to live below the poverty line in retirement.
- Unmarried women (divorced, widowed, never married) are four times more likely than married women to live in poverty.

Some people believe traditional healthcare insurance and Medicare will provide enough financial support for LTC needs. Medicare is health insurance for people age sixty-five or older, or who are entitled to Social Security, or railroad retirement benefits. In limited cases, Medicare may provide some short-term coverage for a nursing home or rehabilitation. To be eligible, the insured must first spend three days in a hospital. Within thirty days from entering the hospital, the insured must enter a Medicare-approved skilled nursing facility. Medicare then pays for costs in part or whole up to the next 100 days, but payment during this period is not guaranteed. Medicare pays the full cost up to the first twenty days and may pay a partial amount for the next eighty days. Once this Medicare assistance ends, you must either self-pay for continued LTC needs or, if the patient has LTC insurance, the insurance company will pay the costs according to the terms and conditions of the policy purchased.

There seem to be two common arguments against preparing for LTC coverage and its cost: 1) the "I will die in my sleep" syndrome, and 2) the "My kids will take care of me" belief. Perhaps some of us are psychic enough to know when and how we will die, but the probability of getting this one right is pretty low. The author's father subscribed to the first syndrome, only one day to have a stroke and spend about eight months in the hospital and a rehabilitation facility. Luckily, he had succumbed to his son's persistence, and only four months before the stroke, he executed an estate plan that enabled his wife to care for him in his time of greatest need.

As for the belief that you may rely on children to take care of you, how many of us genuinely believe family members today will care for us when we need it? It is possible, yet the caregiver usually is a female family member who must, on her own, manage the complicated issues of cost, care, placement, transportation, care for her children and spouse, employment, etc. If relying on family for care is in your game plan, involve the family in the education and planning of what is required. Changing course mid-stream because family reliance is neither feasible, nor acceptable, may only limit options. It is better to handle these issues while you are healthy and have the time to take the best course of action for yourself. So, what are the signs to notice early enough to promulgate a plan and hopefully avoid a hastened response?

SPOTTING DECLINING FACULTIES

First, there may be many declining health signs and options to choose long before a loved one has "an episode." These signs may be physical or mental. The physical signs are more obvious, and assuming a person in need is honest about his or her condition, family can help be proactive. Many people are reluctant to let go of their home, yet their home may be the very thing that hastens their physical decline. If an elderly loved one is not too coordinated, has stairs to traverse at home, or is simply having difficulty being ambulatory, he or she may be at risk at home. One fall may lead to surgery, hospital care along with its viruses, and a stint at a rehabilitation facility, with its additional costs. Women seem especially susceptible to breaking a hip when falling, and too often, they battle a respiratory disease or pneumonia when hospitalized, even succumbing to it all due to a mere fall. During the COVID-19 pandemic, simple falls resulted in death when combined with exposure to the coronavirus in a hospital.

Second, putting aside a clear episode such as a fall or other physical injury/illness, initial cognitive issues may be visible to the watchful eye. Some subtle signs may include forgetfulness, verbal repetition, diminished focus, decreased organization, having trouble with problem solving, and difficulty with driving. The signs may be subtle to the unlearned eye, but if uncovered and if medical assistance is sought early, it could reduce much fear, anxiety, and the chances of a risky visit to a hospital or rehabilitation facility. With declining cognitive issues, appropriate initial management may simply be about how an elderly person handles his or her daily routine.

Let us assume you are a neighbor of Ellen, and since her husband died, you check in on her from time to time. Let us further assume that when you visit her, you notice piles of unopened mail on the kitchen table and counters, including unopened utility bills, shut-off notices, unpaid gap insurance bills, etc. Laundry is not done or neatly folded in its proper place, the house seems cluttered, maybe even with piles of newspapers or magazines in places. Maybe she is not bathing regularly. Ellen may say she is fine; she may even be a wonderful conversationalist and able to hide her forgetfulness, yet dementia has started. She may be forgetting to pay her crucial bills, such as medical insurance coverage, electric, heating, or mortgage bills, to her detriment.

Ellen may also exhibit signs of anxiety. Maybe you notice that her car has more noticeable dings on it or she has had difficulty finding her way home now and then when driving. Perhaps her anxiety with driving has resulted in her denying herself trips to buy food, pharmaceutical needs, or even routine doctor visits. At this stage, her needs may not have attained the level to which medical duties should be taken over by her appointed healthcare agent. Then, again, maybe she has not even appointed one.

Even if Ellen experiences mild cognitive impairment (MCL), it likely will lead to increased stages of dementia, making it important to notice the signs early and seek medical help to reduce stress and prepare for next stages. If these early signs are noticed, Ellen could receive the assistance she needs before the more dangerous effects of her diminished cognition result in her wandering at night or forgetting her way home. Even worse, one client of the author forgot she had food cooking on her gas stove, resulting in a costly and almost fatal house fire before family learned of her decreased cognitive issues. Assistance also could be someone simply helping Ellen with her finances; doing her laundry; cleaning up around the house; making sure she is eating well, properly taking her medications, and bathing regularly; transporting her to doctor appointments; and making grocery and pharmaceutical runs.

Key questions, and often difficult ones to consider for loved ones are: At this stage, is he or she the type of person who would listen to a loved one or trusted friend and welcome assistance? If not, are the symptoms to the level that a guardianship/conservatorship action is warranted? This question leads to the corollary question: Is the child who might be the appointed healthcare agent ready to be the parent to his or her parent? Often, difficult decisions must be made. In some states, a doctor could help if legal authority exists for the doctor to notify the state motor vehicle department and have a physical or cognitive-impaired person's driver's license suspended for not only the patient's protection but also that of the other people on the road. The doctor could examine the patient, determine the extent of his or her diminished cognitive abilities, and provide a clearer picture of the next steps needed. The doctor may refer the loved one to a neurologist or other professional to test his or her cognitive abilities. It is especially important to have such tests performed early to establish a baseline of cognitive ability. The doctor then could compare future cognitive test results to this initial base-line test to chart any degradation in cognitive abilities. This process also helps to prepare the individual and family for future issues they may expect.

A third concern is how stressed the family caregiver might get over time, resulting in unknowingly treating the impaired loved one harshly, either verbally or physically. Verbal abuse due to short tempers and stressed nerves may unwittingly cause a negative situation that could be avoided with day care stays or even other caregivers helping to provide a reprieve to the primary family caregiver.

The best scenario, of course, is preparing for the likelihood for such events well in advance of any initial signs. Be vigilant and plan as if you are one of the 70 percent who will require such care. Communicate with family and discuss the options you would want if such an event occurs. View your living surroundings with different eyes and institute preventative measures or consider alternative living arrangements. The care assistance may be a caregiver, a care coordinator who arranges for your assistance and needs, healthcare services encompassing fitness, nutrition, and other therapy care, a living facility that provides many of these options, or at least a watchful eye to report to such people assisting you. If a medical power/directive were executed, the appointed healthcare agent could speak to the patient's medical personnel for help.

Lastly, at some point, an elder's needs progress beyond health assistance, covered by Medicare, requiring rehabilitation and long-term care assistance. In such cases, LTC will be required. What are the chances that you might need LTC, and how much should you expect it to cost where you live given the care required/desired?

Sometimes people just feel it is their time so they may start organizing or cleaning up their lives in preparation, perhaps to protect family when they leave. Some people feel they are ready. One man who engaged in such activities woke up in the hospital after a stroke and exclaimed to his eldest son, "I want to go." After months lying in the hospital bed, the son thought his father wanted to leave the hospital. After a long pause, the father explained that while he was unconscious, he had met Jesus. This came as a bit of a surprise to the son since the father's favorite joke was to show how a Catholic priest blesses someone, saying, "In the name of the Father, and of the Son, and of the Holy Spirit," and then reaches out his palm and says, "Now show me the money." After a long pause, the father said that when he met Jesus, he told Jesus he was ready to go, but Jesus said, "No, it is not your time." Subsequently, the father explained that afterwards, he had "looked down" at his wife, who was crying in the corner of his hospital room, scared he would leave her. He then said to his son, "I decided then that I would stay." After another long pause, the son asked his father what he now planned to do. His father said, "I guess it's time to get better." The son is your author; the man is his father.

PREPAREDNESS QUESTIONS

1. Are you a member of the Sandwich Generation? If so, what additional help might be best to help you and the person for whom you are caring?

2. What early diminished cognitive or ADLs might you or an elderly loved one be experiencing? What actions could you take to protect yourself or your loved one?

3. If you believe you or an elderly loved one might be experiencing diminished cognitive abilities, or if dementia is a family trait, what actions are you prepared to undertake to protect yourself or your loved one?

CHAPTER FIVE:

Discovering Long-Term Care (LTC) Costs by Region

"All things are ready, if our minds be so."

— William Shakespeare, *Henry V*

As stated in the last chapter, the United States Department of Health and Human Services reports 7 out of 10 people over age sixty-five will require LTC in their lifetime.[19] Given this probability of your needing LTC, are you prepared for the costs? According to a 2018 AARP Bulletin,[20] the out-of-pocket cost is an annual *average* of $140,000 USD. A 2019 Genworth Cost of Care Survey depicts a more thorough report. The average daily and monthly LTC costs for different types of care in the United States from this Cost of Care Survey are as follows.[21]

KNOWING THE U.S. NATIONAL AVERAGE

Home Service:	$143/day	$4,290/month
Home Health Aide:	$146/day	$4,385/month
Adult Day Healthcare:	$54/day	$1,625/month
Asst. Living Facility:	$135/day	$4,051/month
Nursing Home Care		
• Semi-private room:	$250/day	$7,513/month
• Private room:	$284/day	$8,517/month

SEEING REGIONAL DIFFERENCES

For a more expansive picture, following are samples of 2019 average state costs over different regions of the country for various LTC needs, provided in the 2019 Genworth Survey.[22] Since these figures are average state costs, expect to find higher costs in more affluent areas within a state. These figures reflect End-Stage potential costs, so your geographic area for retirement also may play a part in your End-Stage security planning. Consult, therefore, Genworth's survey for costs, and at least know the opportunity cost to "staying where family is." Also notice the difference in home and facility costs among states. Some states focus more on homecare; others focus on nursing or facility care, which are reflected in state Medicaid policies.

(Daily figures rounded)

Northeast

	Connecticut per day/per month	Massachusetts per day/per month	New York per day/per month
Home Service:	$140; $4,195	$173; $5,186	$159; $4,767
Home Health Aide:	$152; $4,576	$175; $5,243	$159; $4,767
Adult Day Health-care:	$ 61; $1,842	$ 49; $1,473	$ 61; $1,842
Asst. Living Facility:	$163; $4,880	$181; $5,640	$232; $6,950
Nursing Home Care			
• Semi-private room	$423; $12,699	$416; $12,473	$387; $12,167
• Private room:	$464; $13,916	$440; $13,212	$448; $13,429

Southeast/Mid-Atlantic

	Florida per day/per month	Virginia per day/per month	North Carolina per day/per month
Home Service:	$133; $4,004	$140; $4,195	$127; $3,813
Home Health Aide:	$140; $4,195	$146; $4,382	$127; $3,813
Adult Day Healthcare:	$ 49 $1,473	$ 53; $1,603	$ 39; $1,170
Asst. Living Facility:	$117; $3,500	$160; $4,800	$133; $4,000
Nursing Home Care			
• Semi-private room	$285; $8,547	$245; $7,350	$235; $7,057
• Private room:	$313; $9,387	$274; $8,213	$256; $7,665

South/Midwest

	Arizona per day/per month	Colorado per day/per month	Texas per day/per month
Home Service:	$159; $4,767	$165; $4,957	$132; $3,956
Home Health Aide:	$159; $4,767	$165; $4,957	$133; $4,004
Adult Day Healthcare:	$ 70; $2,102	$ 54; $1,625	$ 23; $ 704
Asst. Living Facility:	$125; $3,750	$137; $4,095	$125; $3,750
Nursing Home Care			
• Semi-private room	$214; $6,433	$273; $8,197	$162; $4,867
• Private room:	$271; $8,136	$314; $9,429	$214; $6,418

Northwest

	California per day/per month	Oregon per day/per month	Washington per day/per month
Home Service:	$178; $5,335	$172; $5,148	$191; $5,720
Home Health Aide:	$178; $5,339	$178; $5,339	$194; $5,815
Adult Day Healthcare:	$ 56; $1,668	$ 72; $2,167	$ 48; $1,441
Asst. Living Facility:	$150; $4,500	$150; $4,499	$183; $5,500
Nursing Home Care			
• Semi-private room	$292; $8,760	$318; $9,551	$304; $9,112
• Private room:	$355; $10,644	$345; $10,342	$331; $9,931

Consider how many people are ready for the costs and related issues of needing care for themselves and with making care choices for their spouse. Many people believe they have adequate savings to cover any costs associated with LTC. Yet, according to a 2016 Genworth Cost of Care survey, "Americans between the age of 55 and 64 have an estimated $104,000 in their savings accounts."[23] A 2018 AARP study found that most U.S. citizens are unaware of the costs associated with LTC and overestimate the amount that government programs, such as Medicare, will pay. (Also, see Chapter Six on average investments per age group in America.)

How then can you solve this problem and prepare for your End-Stage LTC costs? The answer, and a premise of this book: over time and with careful management of your wealth with a balanced approach of present and later-year needs/wants throughout the many stages of your life. After looking at the different costs for care around the United States, planning for your location in retirement may be just as important a variable for success as how much to allocate in your budget for LTC costs. The following chapter will examine various stages in your life with ways to prepare for the expenses of an End-Stage event along with suggested estate planning considerations.

PREPAREDNESS QUESTIONS

1. In your state of residence, how could you pay for LTC assistance?

2. Have you considered relocating to a state that is more cost-effective for such care, and if so, which state might you consider?

3. Consult websites like Kiplinger.com's State-by-State Guide to Taxes on Retirees and Sperling's Best Places at bestplaces.net to compare taxes and living expenses by state and city.

CHAPTER SIX:

Planning for Life Stages

"If you believe you can accomplish everything by "cramming" at the eleventh hour, by all means, don't lift a finger now. But you may think twice about beginning to build your ark once it has already started raining."

— Max Brooks, *The Zombie Survival Guide: Complete Protection from the Living Dead*

Each stage of your life poses additional and unique challenges to your budget and estate planning needs. This chapter considers the potential duration for LTC needs, the financial challenges with creating your End-Stage security in each life stage, and corresponding changing estate planning needs.

UNDERSTANDING THE COSTS OF YOUR END-STAGE SECURITY

Research conducted by the American Association for Long Term Care Insurance (AALTCI),[24] which used over 2000 claims from years 2000-2011 in its analysis, provides a good picture of lengths of stay in care facilities. The results follow.

For one suffering from **Alzheimer's** who made a claim in his or her early sixties and early seventies:

- 64-65% needed a 3-year stay
- 51-52% a 4-year stay
- 42% a 5-year stay

These figures decreased for claims made by people in their eighties and nineties.

For claims made in one's sixties due to issues with **arthritis**, percentages were higher.

- 81% required a 4-year stay
- 77% required a 5-year stay

Stroke? For claims made in one's early sixties:

- 72% required a 3-year stay
- 64% required a 4-year stay
- 61% required a 5-year stay

For stroke claims made at age seventy-two:

- 66% required a 3-year stay
- 57% required a 4-year stay
- 48% required a 5-year stay

When reading about LTC facility stays, often just three years is reported as the average number of years a person requires, but as the above figures show, some types of medical issues require more time, especially if the need occurs in earlier years. In addition, the reported average of three years may not consider rehabilitation time after an illness; as discussed, Medicare may only provide short-term assistance with rehabilitation. Remember, average duration means 50 percent of people, meaning many people require more years of coverage. Look at the costs in the last chapter for the area in which you live, or plan to live in your retirement, and consider your potential LTC costs. Now let us use a three-year average duration of time for LTC with the average national figures to determine average U.S. LTC costs to provide some general guidance.

For both national home care and home assisted living, average U.S. costs are about $4,000 a month or $48,000 a year. Over three years, that cost equates to $144,000. But a semi-private room is $7,441 a month, close to $90,000 a year, and $270,000 over three years. A private room would cost just over $300,000 for three years. Of the states in the above sampling, Texas looks cheapest; however, for many other states/regions, LTC costs much more. For instance, for the same yearly coverage in Connecticut, these higher figures are: $4,100 a month ($49,200 a year) for homecare; about $151,500 a year for a semi-private room, and about $165,000 a year for a private room. Over a three-year period, that equates to just over $147,500 for homecare, almost $455,000 for a semi-private room, and about $495,000 for a private room.

If we use a five-year duration with national U.S. average figures, the resultant costs are:

Five years of home care or assisted living costs:	$240,000
Five years of semi-private room costs:	$446,460
Five years of private room costs:	$501,900

So, what would you be willing to budget given your age, potential genetic predispositions, and region of the country in which you intend to live in retirement to provide for your and your spouse's End-Stage security? When should you start budgeting? Does it make a difference?

OBTAINING YOUR FIRST JOB—NOW WHAT?

The last thing people in their twenties may consider is not

only the cost of End-Stage security but End-Stage issues themselves. Hopefully, individuals obtaining their first job focus on creating a healthy budget, establishing an emergency fund, eliminating and avoiding debt, and investing. By adding an investment for LTC costs into their consistently maintained budget, they likely will not need to worry about its costs when needed. They truly can create their own grace and security for their future with little financial worry. Looking at retirement investing in this age group, however, provides a sad picture of likely behavioral attitudes toward End-Stage security investing. Few people in this age group adequately invest for even retirement needs. Fidelity Investments reports that the average (mean) balance of 401(k) accounts at Fidelity Investments for its investors in the age group of 20-29 years is just $11,600; the median investment for this age group is a mere $4,000,[25] meaning the sampling is skewed toward the many who invest lower amounts with a few people who invest more to bring up the average. Consider the Personal Wealth formula in Chapter Two—multiply age times wealth divided by ten to determine your wealth—and it is clear that many individuals in their twenties are off to a bad start in creating their financial and End-Stage security.

If you were to plan and allocate in your budget a specific savings amount toward this goal of providing for your End-Stage security, what would it look like? Reference the time-value of money discussion in Chapter Two. Let us start simply with a very conservative investment, thus low risk of loss. If you invested $300 at the beginning of *each month* starting at age twenty-five, given just a 2 percent rate of return, compounded annually, by age seventy, you would yield $262,340 before taxes. However, if this investment were taxed at a combined federal and state marginal income tax rate of 29.5 percent, your net investments would yield $226,375. However, note further the impact of inflation. If you factor in an assumed inflation rate of 2.9 percent over this term, your investment would be further eroded to $62,537 of purchasing power. If the income tax rate and/or inflation rate is lower, your after-tax and post-inflation return would be higher.

If, instead, you invested $400 over the same investment term, you would yield $349,787 before taxes. After the same combined income tax rate, the investment is $301,833 at the end of the term. Factoring in the same 2.9 percent annual inflation rate robs you of purchasing power, to only $83,383. Given the same period to invest and increasing your investment by $100 a month to $500, you increase your after-tax investment results by $75,458. Notice how a slight adjustment to your budget could provide a significant enough benefit with an example of only a conservative investment—one with just a low rate of return of 2 percent.

Now, what if you postponed investing until age forty, using the same parameters as above with a $400 monthly investment? Your pre-tax investment yield would be $197,554, with an after-tax yield of $179,676. The fifteen-year waiting period (starting at age forty instead of twenty-five) results in lost benefits of $122,157. You lost the benefits of time-value of money or compounding due to a shortened investment period. This example shows how procrastination robs you of needed capital later in life. To put it another way, procrastination emphasizes early benefits—tuition, a more pleasurable lifestyle—over End-Stage security.

What if you decided to invest $200 every two weeks, instead of $400 every month? What would be the difference, and would it be significant? Assume again that you started investing $200 every two weeks starting at age twenty-five, all other investing variables as above remaining the same. By age seventy, you would yield $378,200 pre-tax; $326,445 after tax. By investing the same monthly amount but increasing your periodic payments from every month to every two weeks, you increase your investment yield almost $25,000 by the end of the term.

Now, let us investigate a higher rate of return, with thus greater, yet reasonable risk, to create greater investment returns. Assume you invest $400 at the beginning of each month starting at age thirty until age seventy at a rate of return of 5 percent, compounded annually. Your pre-tax investment results would be $598,242; assuming a combined federal and state applicable marginal income tax of 29.5 percent, you would yield $417,548. Compare this figure to the average cost of LTC in your region. It might provide just the right amount of investments needed for your End-Stage security.

However, considering inflationary increases in long-term care costs over time puts further pressure on increasing the rate of return on your investments. A higher rate of return would yield greater results but involve more risk of loss. Likewise, a lower inflation rate and lower applicable marginal income tax rate would increase your investment earnings, meaning government policies also play a factor in your future. Also, consider that if you allocate this investment only for LTC needs and not for retirement living, you likely will have a longer term to invest until an End-Stage event occurs (versus commencing retirement), thus further increasing this investment amount for LTC coverage.

After creating your End-Stage security throughout life, upon retirement you then have the luxury to lower your risk and invest in more conservative investments. You also may choose to use this investment to leverage even higher coverage by purchasing LTC insurance at some point. A choice to invest earlier in life or to contribute a greater allocation of your budget will provide you with the option to self-pay or have the funds to purchase more coverage through long-term care insurance. Yet how many people in their twenties would even read this book or others like it? If you are in this age group and reading this book, you are way ahead of most people and you deserve much credit! With careful planning, and a properly allocated financial plan, you may choose to pursue a higher rate of return with your LTC investment, yet keep in mind that the greater the rate of return, the greater the risk of loss. The key is to consider this issue and its costs as early as possible and plan accordingly. Keep in mind, if you initially plan and maintain a budget, it is easier to maintain the formed habit. The longer you procrastinate, the more difficult it is to allocate the greater sum of money required to catch-up.

This discussion, however, assumes a potential unlikely scenario—that your living costs remain the same (without at least an offsetting increase in pay) during your lifetime. What if you wish to include marriage and children into your life, with the increased living standards (and costs) associated with such choices? What about having funds for a down payment on a home? What about PITA costs, life insurance, and investments for your children's education? The best practice for success: keep and maintain a budget with a priority of maintaining investments toward your End-Stage security.

Your Estate Plan

Another protection to consider is your estate plan. When in your twenties, what would your likely estate plan be? As mentioned before, at least execute a medical directive to appoint the appropriate people to make medical decisions for you if you are ever incapable of doing so. This directive may also include a living will. Do not assume this planning is only for older people. At any time, an accident or debilitating illness/injury could affect you. Do not assume your parents can speak to medical personnel and make decisions for you. Once you become an adult, the HIPAA applies, and without a medical directive, your parents may be forced to go to probate court for the authority to make medical decisions for you. A notorious example of a person without a medical directive was Terry M. Schiavo. She experienced cardiac arrest at age twenty-six and suffered brain damage when revived by life support measures. As a result, she was diagnosed with an irreversible vegetative state. Her husband wanted to remove life support, claiming she would not have wanted to continue in her state of being. Her parents, however, disagreed and challenged her medical prognosis, desiring to keep her on life support. This case became politicized as the U.S. President and Congress weighed in on the issue. Ultimately, the matter went to the Sixth U.S. Circuit Court (a federal court), and after appeals, eventually Terry's life support was removed. A simple medical directive would have avoided this whole situation.

If any discernable wealth has not yet accumulated, perhaps a will at this time is unnecessary. There is a one-size-fits-all intestacy statute in each state that will distribute your wealth among family members. If that is an issue, make a will. Upon accumulating some wealth, savings, investments, or a home, a will and a financial power of attorney likely are in order as well.

At this stage, life insurance may not be a key factor, unless to handle any outstanding debt. You may choose to include it as part of an overall investment plan to enable you to borrow from your own life insurance policy (non-term) instead of borrowing from a bank for future purchases, such as a car, or maybe assistance with a down payment on a home. When using life insurance for future borrowing needs, the interest paid on the loan is usually at a lower rate than it would be from a third-party lender, and the payments benefit your life insurance, not a third-party lender. If you die while any loan is outstanding, the death benefit will be reduced by the loan amount. A carefully chosen life insurance policy may also assist you with End-Stage issues. A good financial planner could assist in this choice.

GETTING MARRIED—CONSIDERING WHAT IS FINANCIALLY AHEAD

Love is love, but since this book is about creating your End-Stage security, before saying "I do," also consider your partner's relationship to money. Money issues are an oft-stated factor in marital failure. Is your partner coming into the marriage with debt, especially credit card debt, thus possibly indicating a lack of a personal budget or discipline maintaining a budget? Will your partner share your desire to provide for End-Stage security, or will your funds that otherwise provide such security go to pay for your partner's poor money management? If so, are you willing to pay for his or her poor lifestyle choices to the detriment of your security later in life? If you have a healthy relationship with money but your partner does not, are you willing to pay for his or her irresponsible financial decisions upon divorce? What about having this anchor of debt throughout your marriage or even upon your partner's death? If your spouse does have debt, consider life insurance on his or her life so you will at least have a death benefit to pay your spouse's debt upon his or her death. Remember family resources allocated to pay the interest on debt robs you not only of that amount that could go toward investments, but the compounding effects as well.

Ideally, both of you will have the same healthy relationship to money ensuring like-minded sacrifices when times are financially difficult and a multiplying beneficial effect during financially healthy times to create financial security throughout your lives. Having the courage and fortitude to create a budget together before marriage (and children) not only will provide a glimpse into the marriage's financial health but also determine whether together you will create financial security and financial happiness. Consider the section on creating a budget in Chapter Two and work out your financial future together. Anticipate increasing costs for housing choices, for children, and whether you both agree to invest for your children's education costs. Determine how your combined earning potential impacts such lifestyle choices. The key is to anticipate and plan for the added stress with money issues and to mind your debt, retirement investments, and End-Stage security. Seek to maintain your determined percentage of net income allocated in your budget toward these categories. Above all, not only *plan*, but be brutally honest with each other with the plan.

Your Estate Plan

At this stage, the same estate planning concerns apply as in the above section; however, you might choose to appoint your spouse as your healthcare agent and attorney-in-fact in your power of attorney (assuming your partner has a healthy relationship with money). Take into consideration that a surviving spouse has a statutory right to inherit a percentage of the deceased spouse's estate upon that partner's death. What if you have some wealth of your own, perhaps from a family inheritance that you (and your family) wish to keep within the family? Without planning, if you should die prior to your spouse, this statutory share would mean your spouse would be able to inherit such wealth and provide for his or her next spouse/family with it. If this is not your intention, consider a prenuptial agreement, and in many states, you will also want to create a revocable trust to preserve your family wealth.

The prenuptial agreement can handle many financial issues during the marriage, upon divorce, and upon death; however, for this issue, it will establish that the wealth each of you have when entering the marriage will not be marital assets in case of divorce. When negotiating a prenuptial agreement, each of you must have your own lawyer and all assets must be disclosed. It should not be negotiated and executed shortly prior to the marriage because that increases the chance it may not be honored in court. A prenuptial agreement is conditioned upon marriage. The closer to the wedding date it is signed, the more it looks like one side may have been pressured to enter into the agreement.

Along with the prenuptial agreement, creating a revocable trust and funding it with your pre-marital wealth (not intended to be commingled with the marital assets) also establishes to a judge in a divorce action that you clearly intended to segregate such assets from the marriage. Consulting a lawyer in your state is essential since property rights, divorce laws, and inheritance laws vary from state to state.

Lastly, if debt is incurred (such as a note/mortgage for the purchase of a home), consult the life insurance section of Chapter

Two. Determine the loss of income from the death of a spouse when the budget considers two incomes to sustain it and the likely debt that life insurance otherwise could eliminate to ease the surviving spouse's financial burden.

HAVING CHILDREN—THEY COST HOW MUCH?

The average (mean) balance of 401(k) accounts at Fidelity Investments for Fidelity investors in the 30-39 age group is $43,600, and the median investment for this age group has a balance of $16,500, far short of healthy retirement preparedness. For Fidelity investors in the 40-49 age group, the mean balance is $106,200, and the median investment has a balance of $36,900. Besides poor planning, and the potential budgetary strain to make healthy investments for investors in these age groups, the additional costs of children must be considered.

According to the U.S. Department of Agriculture, it costs (for food, shelter, and other necessities) an average of $233,610 (in 2015 dollars) to raise a child until age seventeen for a middle-income, married-couple family with two children.[26] Not surprisingly, the study states that "married-couple families in the urban Northeast have the highest child rearing expenses." The study also concludes that child-rearing expenses are about the same for a single parent household below middle class.

Add to the essential costs above the other expenses associated with a child: toys, medical costs, school costs (not just college), extra activities in sports and music, travel costs, loss of work on holidays, sick days, etc., and the cost is astounding. In addition, factor in extra costs associated with your children staying home later in life compared to previous generations. Then decide if you choose to invest for your child's college costs, and if so, how much you must invest to accomplish your determined goal for this purpose. Adjust your budget accordingly. Factoring these costs into your budget not only provides a balanced financial approach to raising a family, but it helps you keep your own future needs in focus, which must also be considered.

As for paying your children's college costs, some people believe it is worth paying the high tuition costs of Ivy and baby Ivy League colleges and universities. Higher education is an important factor that enhances one's income level. But consider the costs, both to you and your child, especially given your child's intended field of study. Many college students initially dream of specializing in challenging high-paying fields, like engineering or pre-medical courses, only to change their major at some point. Many undergraduate universities, especially state universities and those in the southern and mid-section of the country, provide the same education for non-specialized degrees, but for less cost. There may be no need to pay high-end university costs for a degree that could be achieved at any other university. Graduate programs tend to focus a person's career path, especially the higher-paying occupations. If children achieve on the undergraduate level, then they can strive for the graduate school that best meets the field in which they choose to specialize. Mortgaging your, or your child's, future for an Ivy League diploma may retard your success. Although it may help your child, there is no guarantee of that either. Factor you and your spouse into the equation. Consider in such decision-making how well you provided for yourselves for retirement and your End-Stage security. Also, consider how much you have invested toward your child's university studies to pay toward the costs. Adding debt may be the worst thing—for your own future—and send a poor message to your child. Stay balanced in your financial and life choices.

Since the financial recession of 2008, more children have chosen to live at home with their parents post-college than in past generations. Should their housing, food, cell phone, clothes, etc. be paid by you, the parent? This is a great opportunity to teach them how to create and balance their budget for when they fly the home nest. Teach them to be accountable for their desires and expenses. Charge them a reasonable rent. You can always invest it and later give it to them as a security deposit on a new rent or help with a deposit on the purchase of a home. If you can afford it, buy a life insurance policy on their life for them to own that builds cash; maybe share the premium costs with them to teach them investing as well as how to build some cash for their future needs and financial security.

Likely Estate Plan

Now that you have brought children into the mix, create guardianship designations. In some states, this appointment may be done with a stand-alone document; in others, it will be a provision in your will. The biological parent has the presumption of parental/guardian duties. The guardianship appointment is in case there is no surviving spouse, or the surviving spouse is unable to handle such duties. Your will should be changed to include your children, although many states have statutory provisions to include children born after the execution of a will, and in intestacy statutes if there is no will.

The next issue is at what age you think your children should inherit your wealth and will manage it appropriately. States have enacted a statute that allows for assets that a minor inherits to be held in a custodial account, called a Uniform Gift to Minors Act (UGMA) or Uniform Transfer to Minors Act (UTMA). These accounts are subject to probate court supervision. The longest you can keep assets in the custodial account for the benefit of a minor child is to age eighteen or twenty-one, hardly old enough or mature enough to handle an inheritance. For this reason, consider either creating a trust in your will (called a testamentary trust), or creating a stand-alone (an inter-vivos or revocable) trust in case a child is too young or immature to inherit wealth when the time comes. Also, factor the issues presented in the following section involving a dissolution of marriage. Would you want your child's ex-spouse to get the proverbial half of your child's wealth in a divorce, which he or she inherited from you? If you die and have a will that gives your child a share of your wealth outright, and your child has a divorce subsequently, this may happen. Consider in your estate plan having assets held in trust for the benefit of your child until an age when you feel he or she not only might be mature enough to manage wealth but also will have a stable marriage. Assets held in a properly drafted trust should shield such inheritance from a divorce action, yet still provide income or principal from the trust for your child's benefit. Creating a (testamentary) trust in your will entails probate court oversight, accounting reports, and probate fees. A revocable trust may involve a slightly higher up-front cost for a lawyer to draft it, but it avoids continuing probate involvement and costs.

What might this child's trust look like? Some factors to consider are how a child manages wealth/finances, the child's maturity, and when you expect the child will consider they will not live forever and choose to face their own retirement and End-Stage security needs. Also consider that along with children staying at home longer, they also are marrying later, followed by divorcing at later ages. A receipt of sizable wealth before this determined age of maturity, marriage, or divorce, which is likely after age thirty, and for some maybe never, requires holding assets in trust throughout a child's life.

While assets are held in trust, the trustee could provide income and principal distributions of the trust assets to the child for reasons you determine, commonly for health, education, and living expenses (up to a certain age). Perhaps a percentage of the assets may also be distributed each year or even just one time. Many options exist when considering distributing the income and principal of trust assets, including whether to do so, and if so, when, and then how to wind down the trust by distributing out the principal. For example, the author's estate plan for his daughter entails providing income and principal for her health, education, and living expenses until she attains age twenty-three, and thereafter, for just health and education expenses and winding down the trust by providing her with the option to withdraw one quarter of the then-existing balance at ages thirty, thirty-five, and forty, and then the remaining trust balance at forty-five. When she was about to leave for college, her father showed her the estate plan and explained that no matter what happened in life, she was protected, but if her father did not like the guy she fell in love with, she might never get trust funds outright. To her credit, she was unfazed. Another popular winding down option is to provide smaller withdrawal amounts at earlier ages, increasing such amounts as the child gets older. A good estate planning attorney could discuss the many variables you need to consider what is best for your family.

Lastly, revisit your life insurance needs to consider replacing the loss of income of each parent upon death and the debt, college costs, legacy desires, and even child-rearing costs necessary after the death of you or your partner. If necessary, revisit the section on life insurance in Chapter Two. Transferring the risks of these costs may be critical to ensuring your continued standard of living and the educational goals for your children.

TRANSITIONING—DIVORCE

No one enters a marriage planning for its end (pre-nuptial agreements aside). Yet we often hear that somewhere around half of marriages end in divorce. Since the 1980s, this figure appears to be dropping to around a present figure of 42-45 percent of marriages in the United States.[27] Regardless of the exact percentage, a divorce is significant enough to consider its effects, such as stress, its duration of time, financial impact, division of assets, and efforts to transition to post-divorce life. Average cost for a divorce varies by region and the couple's specific situation. Mediation is cheaper; a long, protracted battle over child custody or division of marital assets is costly. Ancillary costs are the emotional strain on your life, the divorce's effect upon relationships, and even lost time at work. Financially, what a couple once managed together, now one person must do solely. How will you handle a possible division of marital debt in a divorce action? How will it affect your budget and End-Stage security plans? As part of the divorce process, it would be wise to consult a financial planner or estate planning attorney before entering into an agreement to understand the financial impact that would befall you. Understanding the estate planning and money concepts in Chapter Two may also help.

Many divorcing couples have chosen mediators to handle the divorce process, not only to limit costs but to diminish an otherwise very adversarial process. As Sylvia Guinan, author of *The Richness of Divorce: 7 Steps to Unwind Your Marriage with Love and Grace* and a financial professional for the past twenty years at two major U.S. investment brokerage firms, states: "I truly believe that as a society, if we changed the way we look at divorce we can make it a much more amicable process. I am a firm believer that if the divorce process is handled with love and grace, it will ultimately benefit the couple financially, emotionally and most importantly help their children adjust better during this difficult transition process."[28] In addition, with "eyes wide open" when entering the marriage, especially as to financial and estate planning matters, the divorce process could be far less adversarial. When facing divorce, investigate what your finances will be post-judgment before signing any agreement. Then reanalyze your budget.

Likely Estate Plan

In many states, you may not change beneficiary designations for health insurance, investments, etc. once the divorce (dissolution) action commences. This also includes changing your estate planning documents. Once it is permissive by law to change your estate plan, do so. Some states may void a will after a divorce, leaving you with no will at all. Other states only void the provisions that pertain to the ex-spouse, which may make the will ineffective depending on how it was drafted. Also, consider changing your medical and financial powers if you appointed your ex-spouse to handle such matters. Again, some states may by law void these appointments or documents. Regardless, revisit your estate plan as soon as possible when facing divorce.

Since, once divorced, your desired estate plan likely will not provide for all assets passing to your ex-spouse, then to children, it may be a good time to consider a trust, if one is not already part of your estate plan. By using a trust, upon your death, your assets will be held in trust for the benefit of each child pursuant to the terms and conditions you choose when you create the trust, instead of giving the assets (as with a will) outright to the child whom you may consider too young, vulnerable, or immature to manage an inheritance. You could simply hold assets in trust until a certain age when you believe your child will be able to manage assets free of trust. Your chosen trustee will manage and distribute the trust assets for each child according to your distribution desires, as drafted by your attorney. Revisit Chapter Three for a fuller discussion on this topic.

Besides changing your appointed "agent" for your will, trust, healthcare documents, and power of attorney, you also may want to change your desired guardian for your children. In many states, the inference for a guardian is the surviving biological parent absent, unfit circumstances such as substance abuse, or physical or cognitive inabilities. Your guardianship appointment certainly expresses whom you wish to raise any minor child if you are the last parent to die.

Lastly, review your designated beneficiaries of qualified funds (IRAs, 401(k), etc.) as well as life insurance policies. Be mindful of having your children as outright beneficiaries. You may choose to have the designated beneficiary for these assets be your trust for the many reasons discussed above. You also may need to reconsider past life insurance needs and coverage given your change in financial circumstances.

RETIRING AND END-STAGE

The average (mean) balance of 401(k) accounts at Fidelity Investments for their investors for the 50-59 age group is $179,100, and the median investment is $62,700. Yes, at this stage, paying off mortgage debt, if not done so already, may be a paramount focus, although with low prevalent mortgage rates, many financial planners would advise investing in a well-balanced portfolio with higher rates of return than investing in reducing mortgage debt with a low interest rate. Our later fifties seems to be the sweet spot for investigating and purchasing LTC insurance too. Yet, given the above data, besides being unprepared for retirement, few people in this group are prepared to pay for LTC costs, or even LTC insurance.

The average (mean) balance of 401(k) accounts at Fidelity Investments for their investors for the 60-69 age group years is $198,600, and the median investment is just $63,000. This age group is no better prepared for LTC costs than the previous age groups. Add the increased costs of LTC insurance for people in this age group, the effect of self-paying for LTC costs until they are exhausted, and then applying for Medicaid, if then eligible, and the likely financial security outlook for these individuals is not promising.

Relying solely on Social Security benefits likely is not

enough for your living and End-Stage needs, but knowing when to apply for such benefits and the corresponding benefit that you would receive at your age of applying is critical in your retirement planning. Consult the Social Security Administration website at https://www.ssa.gov/myaccount for the exact minimum age you may withdraw Social Security benefits. The website also allows you to determine the likely amount you would receive at different ages when you might withdraw such benefits. Seek guidance on whether it is better for you to wait until you may withdraw full benefits or at an earlier permissible time given your financial situation. According to the Social Security Administration, the first Baby Boomers may withdraw full Social Security benefits at age sixty-six. This age of withdrawal gradually increases until those born after 1960 who may withdraw full benefits at age sixty-seven. Given the apparent strain on Social Security benefits, the legislature may increase these minimal ages over time. Also, consider the present expected decrease in Social Security benefits, as discussed in Chapter Eleven.

Alexandria Bova, in her article "Here's Exactly How Much You Need to Retire in Your State,"[29] determines the amount you would need to live in retirement for each state by deducting Social Security income and assuming a 4 percent annual reduction in investment/savings for living expenses. The report uses Bureau of Labor Statistics and Missouri Economic Research and Information Center data. As you may predict, states in the south are less costly to live in, while states in the northeast are more costly (although Hawaii came in as the most expensive state to retire in, with California and Oregon joining the Northeastern states). Mississippi, Oklahoma, and Arkansas were the least costly, with needed savings of $666,772, $687,116, and $697,288, respectively. In the middle of the list, Illinois (22nd), Utah (24th), and Florida (27th) cost $804,094, $815,537, and $843,537, respectively. The most costly states are New Jersey (42nd) coming in at $1,174,100, Connecticut (43rd) at $1,184,272, Maryland (45th) at $1,238,947, Massachusetts (46th) at $1,249,119, New York (47th) at $1,308,879, Oregon (48th) at $1,334,309, California (49th) at $1,369,911, and Hawaii (50th) at $2,151,884. Given these estimated costs of living in retirement, are you prepared? What about for your End-Stage security? If you are unprepared for such costs, consider Ellen's situation as discussed at the end of this chapter.

As part of your retirement plans, consider both your income and expenses. Relocating to a state that is less costly may be a key variable as well. Also, consider the costs and services of LTC in a state. (See Chapters Four and Five on LTC.)

Your Likely Estate Plan

After the children have finally left home, college tuition

payments are finished, and you start wondering about what retirement might look like financially, it is also a good time to look at your estate plan. The people you appointed when the children were young may not be the same people you wish to rely upon now. For one, those people may be older, have different living or health situations, or no longer be central figures in your life. This is also a time to discuss the LTC and elder issues with a good estate planning attorney and adjust your estate plan according to your, and your family's, changed circumstances, the amount of retirement (and LTC) savings you now have, and where you might move in retirement. By this time, you will have a different perspective on how your children will handle any legacy you pass on to them and the other influences upon their lives in handling wealth. Your late fifties and early sixties are a good time to reassess your investment/savings, especially for LTC needs, and shop around for the best LTC plan that fits your needs.

You also might consider another look at your life insurance policies and needs. At this stage, debt may be far less than when you purchased your life insurance policies—certainly, college debt, but also home financing debt (mortgage). LTC may be the leading concern over debt repayment upon death. The solution may be to shift any permanent (non-term) life insurance to LTC insurance, hybrid LTC, and/or a smaller life insurance policy, or even to obtain a rider on existing life insurance to cover LTC needs. The "shift" may be dropping an older policy and obtaining a new policy or policies; however, it may be an exchange of your old policy for a new one that fits your changing needs. This exchange is commonly called a like-kind exchange or an IRC §1035 exchange. The advantage of this type of exchange is to avoid any capital gains (income) tax associated with terminating an older policy as well as a possible reduced cost to make the exchange as opposed to keeping the existing life insurance and purchasing a LTC insurance policy. Consider at this stage also having a thorough discussion with a financial planner or long-term care specialist of the possible options available.

TAKEAWAY

The key to providing End-Stage security is to establish wise financial goals and budgets at an early age, stay disciplined, and make life choices within such goals with "tune-ups" throughout your life, preferably with key professional advisers, at each stage of your life.

ELLEN'S CASE

Although Ellen and Bob lived comfortably, they did not prepare for their End-Stage security. Many people must navigate alone through the many complicated choices when handling an abrupt change in circumstances because a spouse becomes gravely ill—in Ellen's case, her husband's stroke. In such cases, many people who offer to help have limited knowledge with which to handle the many areas required for the new situation. The many messages, though well intended, further confuse an already complicated situation. Imagine how difficult it would be without a spouse to assist when such illness befalls you. Bob and Ellen did not share their finances; they did not have an adequate estate plan, especially a medical directive or a financial power so Ellen could use their finances held in Bob's name; nor did they choose LTC insurance for when the fateful event occurred.

Fortunately, Ellen availed herself of a life-care planner to assist her, who in turn advised her to speak to a lawyer who knew estate planning and elder law matters. If, at some point, Bob's doctor determines Bob has the cognitive capacity to sign estate planning documents, he could execute a medical directive so Ellen could make medical decisions for him and be his spokesman with his doctors. Likewise, he could execute a power of attorney so Ellen could access his bank accounts, and other assets, in his name. If Bob does not have the requisite capacity to sign such documents, she will need probate authority to act for him through a conservatorship action. The power of attorney will enable her to handle their home finances without a guardian/conservatorship action and pay for their additional needs, such as making their home safe for him to return to or pay for a facility for him to recover in and perhaps stay in afterwards. If he returns home, caregivers will also need to be paid. Yet, without having handled such matters before, how prepared is Ellen to handle them now? Such issues could have been confusing without the sudden occurrence of the stroke. Sharing home finances, handling estate planning needs throughout a couple's lives, and learning about End-Stage security issues all could help prepare someone like Ellen not only to limit the confusing issues presenting themselves to her, but also to help her be more prepared mentally for the event. See Chapter Eight for a fuller discussion on how to handle her Medicaid planning.

Imagine if Bob and Ellen had already met with a lawyer and had a medical directive and financial power of attorney. Imagine further that they met with a financial or LTC advisor who explained how to pay for LTC expenses. They could have been informed together so they could decide whether to purchase LTC insurance or create an investment plan within their budget to self-pay for such costs. As they aged, if they had permanent life insurance and had less need for it, they could have converted it into a LTC insurance policy or a hybrid LTC insurance policy. They also could address with their advisors how and when to apply for Social Security benefits. They might even plan to relocate to an area where living expenses and LTC costs are cheaper. They could have taken their time to investigate and choose a facility to go to when a debilitating illness occurred, maybe even choose what type of living situation they both would have where such services are on-site. In other words, either one of them would be much better prepared to take care of the other when such an event occurred.

With advance knowledge and planning, Bob and Ellen could have determined how to handle the issues they now face when they both were healthy and able to plan carefully for the End-Stage issues, instead of engaging in crisis planning, as Ellen now must do, essentially alone.

PREPAREDNESS QUESTIONS

1. What is your present net worth, and how does it compare to what it should be according to the formula from the authors of *The Millionaire Next Door* (discussed in Chapter Two under "Wealth and Net Worth")? How might you alter your budget to attain this net worth goal?

2. What is your projected net worth at retirement, and is it enough to provide for both your retirement and End-Stage security?

3. After reading this chapter, how might you change your estate plan?

4. After reviewing the Social Security site mentioned in this chapter (https://www.ssa.gov/myaccount), how much Social Security do you estimate you will receive? Given your budget, net worth, retirement savings, and End-Stage expectations, when might you plan to collect Social Security benefits?

5. Do you have life insurance, and will you be able to convert it to a LTC insurance policy later in life? If not, what actions might you take now to have this opportunity?

CHAPTER SEVEN:

SPOTTING FINANCIAL ELDER ABUSE

"An ounce of prevention is worth a pound of cure."

— Benjamin Franklin

Once a person experiences cognitive or physical decline, without adequate supervision they become vulnerable to elder abuse. People in an elder's life must identify elder abuse, be aware of situations ripe for creating it, and of governmental agencies available to assist if a situation should arise. Many areas fall under the category of elder abuse. Following are categories encompassing elder abuse and neglect, which may overlap:

- Physical abuse
- Emotional or Psychological abuse
- Sexual abuse
- Financial abuse

To discuss all the above abuses would be too voluminous for this book. The focus of this chapter, therefore, will be on financial abuse and ways to guard against it, but this in no way diminishes the severity of the other forms of abuse. Sources for assistance are listed throughout this chapter for you to investigate further, if needed.

Since the beginning of the baby boom, the United States has embraced this generation from initially building more parks and schools to a plethora of marketing to sell products to them throughout their lives. This attention has waned, however, for baby boomers who have begun entering their advanced years. Investment firms may have targeted them to manage their wealth for retirement, but society (including its laws on protection) has been slow to address the challenges and vulnerabilities of baby boomers' later years. However, in the last decade or two, elder abuse increasingly has captured the attention of legal and professional organizations, resulting in numerous studies and ensuing legal changes. Protection has been slow, and it varies state-to-state.

LEARNING ABOUT FINANCIAL ABUSE

In 2011, MetLife Mature Market Institute, the National Committee for the Prevention of Elder Abuse (NCPEA), and the Center for Gerontology at Virginia Polytechnic Institute and State

University, released a report called *The MetLife Study of Elder Financial Abuse: Crimes of Occasion, Desperation and Predation Against America's Elders.*[30] It revealed a bleak picture. The study estimated the national cost of elder financial abuse at $2.9 billion annually. It stated that women are at twice the risk of men, and some type of deceit or emotional manipulation is generally employed, sometimes leading to other forms of abuse. Its message: "despite growing public awareness from a parade of high-profile financial abuse victims, it remains under-reported, under-recognized, and under-prosecuted."[31]

Elder financial abuse has three over-riding issues: 1) the age one is considered an elder, 2) the definition of elder financial abuse, and 3) the reporting of such abuse. AARP opens membership at age fifty.[32] The Elder Justice Act (EJA)[33] and the Centers for Disease Control and Prevention (CDC)[34] define an elder as a person sixty years of age or older. The Office for Older Americans[35] uses age sixty-two. State statutes that protect elders use ages between sixty and sixty-five. It depends, therefore, upon which laws are applicable to an issue, and in many cases, in which state the victim lives to determine if a person is a protected "elder" under the law.

In general, elder financial abuse deals with some type of unlawful, deceitful, or manipulative taking of an elder's property. The National Center on Elder Abuse (NCEA) defines elder financial abuse as the "illegal taking, misuse, or concealment of funds, property, or assets of a vulnerable elder."[36] The federal Older Americans Act defines exploitation as the "fraudulent or otherwise illegal, unauthorized, or improper act or process of an individual, including a caregiver or fiduciary, that uses the resources of an older individual for monetary or personal benefit, profit, or gain, or that results in depriving an older individual of rightful access to, or use of, benefits, resources, belongings, or assets."[37] State statutes also have varying definitions. Simply ascertaining the standard for elder financial abuse thus involves careful review of the applicable laws. For an elder, perhaps with diminished cognitive capacity, this task is daunting. Even a concerned family member may find the endeavor a steep and complicated challenge, a factor that alone may account for the under-reporting of elder financial abuse.

What can you do if an elder loved one may have experienced financial abuse? Often the abuse is a crime such as theft, fraud, deception, larceny, forgery, or embezzlement. So, the first option may be to contact the police and report the incident. Contact criminal justice agents or social service personnel who may assist with the complications of pursuing justice. Search for your state's agency on the protection of elders.

After investigating protection laws for seniors, the next disconcerting issue is the under-reporting of abuse. Besides being dependent on family or other caregivers, many victims are socially isolated, even lonely. Many federal acts and state statutes establish mandatory reporting agents, such as banks, lawyers, elder facilities, medical personnel, etc. Nevertheless, many studies and sources, including the Centers for Disease Control (CDC) and U.S. Department of Justice, report that many incidents of elder financial abuse are not reported because of dependence on the perpetrator, diminished cognitive faculties, or various emotions such as fear, shame, and guilt. The National Adult Protective Services Association (NAPSA) reports that 90 percent of perpetrators are family members or individuals whom the elder believed to be trustworthy, such as neighbors, church members, caregivers, or anyone else who presents him- or herself as helping the elder. The National Council on Aging claims that as many as 6 out of 10 abusers are family members,[38] and an overwhelming majority of perpetrators are male.

When caught, the perpetrators often argue that the "gifts" of money are loans that they would repay and that there was no intent to steal. To complicate claims against perpetrators, the abused elder may not be able to explain competently the crime to police or legal reporters for them to adequately pursue the matter. Decreased cognitive ability appears to be a key factor. According to an article by The Gerontological Society of America:[39]

> Fraud and financial exploitation victims performed poorly on tests of cognitive functioning and financial decision making administered by a forensic neuropsychologist following the allegations. Based on retrospective record review, there were few significant differences in physical health and cognitive functioning at the time victims' assets were taken, although their social contexts were different. Significantly more fraud victims were childless compared with financial exploitation victims.

The key, then, for reporting agents and family members is to perceive an elder's potential vulnerability to financial abuse before the abuse occurs. So, what may be some signs to watch for an elder's vulnerability to financial abuses in order to detect and prevent the abuse? The following is a non-exhaustive list to consider.

- Inattention to important mail, such as property tax bills, health insurance invoices, bank withdrawal notices, utility bills, mortgage invoices, or even eviction notices.
- Strange bank account activity, such as atypical transfers and withdrawals, especially with ATM activity.
- New people in their lives, usually claiming to help.
- Changes in estate planning documents, especially powers of attorney or deeds to the home.

- Unusual concern by caregivers or new helpers about the elder's financial situation.
- Missing items in the home, either checkbooks, missing checks out of sequence, jewelry, cash, or other tangible items.
- Signatures on documents or checks that are dissimilar to the elder's usual signature.
- The elder's confusion about or unusual attention to his or her financial affairs.
- A sudden concern to help financially a caregiver or his or her children.
- A new lawyer in the elder's life.

Another important aspect implicit in observing emerging negative factors indicative of financial abuse is the living proximity of family members to the elder and the extent of other reporting agents in the elder's life. Having a family member who lives close to an elder who lives alone, which more often is a daughter or daughter-in-law, and who regularly visits and assists the elder with financial concerns, dramatically increases the probability of early detection. This detection may be either directly or through helping the elder avail him- or herself of others who might also assist in the detection, such as bank tellers, healthcare professionals, a care provider, or even the elder's lawyer.

Perhaps the best means to avoid abuse is proactive planning and appointing people who will be there to assist honestly and thus ward off any abuse. Even living in a Continuing Care Facility instead of alone may help avoid financial abuse. So, how may one adequately plan to avoid this scenario, especially if dementia is in a person's family history?

ELLEN'S CASE

What if Bob and Ellen had routinely met with their estate planning lawyer to update and review their estate plan given their changing circumstances, as discussed in the last chapter? In such a case, they would have had an estate plan that would at least have allowed Ellen to access all of her and Bob's finances to manage them when Bob had his stroke—whether assets were jointly owned, held in trust with successor trustees appointed, or through a proper power of attorney. A good estate planning lawyer would even encourage the sharing of their finances between them so they would be better prepared for an End-Stage event. The lawyer also would have a candid discussion about who they should appoint as their attorney-in-fact for their financial power of attorney or the successor trustees of their trust. This attorney, with a developed relationship not only with Bob and Ellen, but with their appointed financial and medical agents, might be a mandatory reporter of abuse, depending upon the state, and could more quickly and adequately support Ellen when the first signs of need arose. However, candidly, someone closer to Ellen likely would be the first person to notice vulnerable signs and contact the lawyer. With a well-developed plan in place, the lawyer could then quickly act to protect her.

Assume Ellen and her daughter made an appointment with Ellen's estate planning lawyer to change her power of attorney to provide that her daughter alone would be Ellen's attorney-in-fact. The lawyer, especially knowing Ellen and Bob's family dynamics, could observe the relationship Ellen has with her daughter. For instance, is Ellen reliant upon the daughter to drive Ellen to the grocery store and to appointments with health-care professionals and doctors? In the meeting, is the daughter doing all the talking and dictating what she wants? Has Ellen's demeanor changed such that she appears to be more dependent and submissive to her daughter? Does Ellen have any bruises on her body? Is her daughter argumentative or verbally controlling toward Ellen, especially when she believes they are alone? In addition, a careful lawyer should meet privately with Ellen and have a candid conversation with her about changing her and her husband's carefully planned estate plan. The lawyer may ask Ellen questions about the past and the present to glean Ellen's cognitive capacity, not only to make a thoughtful decision to appoint her daughter, but also to determine if she has capacity to execute new estate planning documents. If her cognitive ability is in doubt, the lawyer should ask Ellen to visit her doctor to determine her mental capacity and have the doctor state in writing if Ellen has the requisite mental capacity to sign new estate planning documents. If, after observing Ellen, the doctor concludes she does not have the requisite mental capacity, such determination now is in her record. This record may be used in the future in case her daughter, in turn, tries to bring Ellen to her own chosen lawyer to have her appointed as Ellen's attorney-in-fact. Yes, Ellen's daughter may dissuade Ellen from visiting her doctor in the first place. If the lawyer is not a mandatory reporting agent, his or her efforts to assist Ellen in such a case may be hampered due to the lawyer's duty of confidentiality to his client, Ellen. Hopefully, the new lawyer will be ethical and employ the same careful review of Ellen's situation, but this ethical precaution is not guaranteed.

If Ellen does visit her doctor and it is determined that she has diminished cognitive abilities, such that she cannot handle her financial affairs, and if she has not executed a power of attorney or healthcare document, a family member or other concerned person (even the state) could bring a guardianship/conservatorship action in order to appoint a conservator for Ellen. In such a case, a judge will determine who is the best person to assist Ellen, hopefully avoiding future abuse by Ellen's daughter, son-in-law, or anyone else since then any activities by the appointed conservator will involve court oversight.

PREPAREDNESS QUESTIONS

1. Might you or a loved one be vulnerable to financial abuse, and if so, what actions will you take to avoid its occurrence?

2. Is your estate plan adequate to protect you, and does it appoint the best people to assist you when the need arises?

3. Research and compile a list of resources in your state to assist you and your care providers in case you might be a victim of elder abuse. Keep this list with your estate planning documents.

CHAPTER EIGHT:

UNDERSTANDING PLACE OF CARE AND LONG-TERM CARE INSURANCE

"You cannot escape the responsibility of tomorrow by evading it today."

— Abraham Lincoln

This chapter examines housing considerations. Staying at home with family assistance may not be a viable option for some elders. There are issues to observe that may point toward a need for facility care. The chapter discusses types of typical facility living; however, such care often involves additional cost. For this reason, LTC insurance options and ways to obtain them are also discussed.

LEARNING ABOUT AGING IN PLACE—STAYING AT HOME

One of the most often heard statements by estate and elder planners is: "I don't want to go to a nursing home—I want to remain in my home!" Although staying at home may provide emotional comfort and be the preference of many elders, financial and health concerns must be considered. An elder living alone and isolated from someone who could provide a watchful eye over them is a major factor in elder abuse. In such a situation, alternate living should be considered. The key is to educate yourself, and loved ones, well in advance of the need of the many options available. This education enables you, your family, and a care provider to determine all of the qualitative and quantitative factors involved so that when staying at home is not a viable option, the individual and family are not in crisis mode to determine the perhaps limited quick housing and care options then available. Waiting lists at the more desired residencies may force the family to make less than desirable choices when in crisis mode. You never know when or what circumstances might arise that limit such options. For instance, during the COVID-19 pandemic, nursing homes and other care facilities halted not only visits to their facilities, but severely limited, even halted, the entrance of new residents. What if you were the caregiver in such a case and you were no longer able to adequately plan an elder's housing needs? You might not be able to place the elder in a facility or even be able to visit facilities to place a loved one, thus adding to your stress and fatigue, and exposing the elder to additional harm.

1. **Assistance Needs—Safety Concerns.** Putting aside life-changing illnesses such as dementia, cancer, and heart disease, what occurrences should you anticipate over time? General aging issues must be considered and planned for. As we get older, our bones shrink and become less dense. Our muscles decrease in strength and flexibility. We, thus, experience decreased coordination and balance. As a result, elders tend to be more susceptible to falls and injury, especially broken hips for women. One fall could change the whole paradigm of health, long-term care needs, and even housing desires. What if the caregiver, a spouse perhaps, broke her hip or required hospitalization? Who, then, would provide the caregiving? In addition, hospitalization exposes us to numerous harmful bacteria and viruses, although one seems common to the elderly—Hospital Acquired Pneumonia (HAP).[40] A simple fall may lead to the additional complications of a prolonged nagging illness in conjunction with the underlying rehabilitation. Such a situation causes not only increased hospital stays, but also potential increases in financial costs. As previously mentioned, Medicare assistance covers healthcare. Rehabilitation often leads to a need for long-term care, which for the unpre-

pared is life-changing and costly because Medicare provides limited help at best.

Besides the long-term care costs, safe housing after the rehabilitation period becomes an issue. Is the home conducive to someone with decreased mobility or cognition? Is there adequate assistance at home, especially for mobility needs? Often a home assessment is required before a patient is released from institutional care, resulting in a need for home modifications such as a ramp to enter the home, installation of safety bars in the bathroom, space to maneuver a walker or wheelchair, and perhaps even a stairlift. Internal stairways may be so problematic that a first-floor bedroom must be built or a room remodeled. Additionally, older patients sometimes experience increased confusion after an episode, and changed living arrangements compound the issue. Would living at home in such instances result in increased isolation or depression? At this stage, family members, stressed and concerned over the sudden increased needs of their parent or loved one, require education on options. A glaring question is: Might a facility other than the home be a better choice, especially looking at future aging issues, or is it cost-effective to pay for home modifications and stay at home under the circumstances?

2. **Malnutrition.** With decreased social activity or isolation due to living alone, the elderly tend to prepare food differently. No

longer does it seem worthwhile to prepare full meals. Add financial constraints and decreased ability to go food shopping, such as difficulties with driving, and food intake sometimes becomes inadequate. More importantly, who is there to monitor the elder to make sure he or she is eating appropriately, especially if the elder is experiencing memory loss? Perhaps paying for outside services to provide meals would solve the issue, but for how long?

3. **Home Maintenance.** As we get older, those cumbersome home and yard maintenance issues either get ignored or put the elderly at risk to accomplish them. Cleaning gutters, clearing leaves in autumn, shoveling snow, and dealing with ice in the winter, or even maintaining household mechanicals, such as the furnace, water heater, and air-conditioning units, becomes problematic. Financially preparing in advance for these events and having someone to assist with these chores makes all the difference. Issues surrounding living in isolation as discussed in Chapter Seven about financial elder abuse may also dissuade you from staying at home. Attitude toward change, often expressed as "not yet being ready," appears to be the biggest obstacle. The more advance planning you pursue, the easier it will be to make this difficult but crucial decision. Sometimes the family caregiver must make the decision, in which case the next question becomes: Is the caregiver ready

for the change?

4. **Money Management.** As we age, our cognitive abilities decrease. Add dementia to the mix and the elderly easily get confused over not only simple tasks such as balancing a checkbook and paying bills, but the complicated matters in their lives like handling Social Security, Medicare, and health forms. There certainly are exceptions. Too often, however, children find piles of mail on their elderly parent's kitchen table and counters, only to find that payment for important services, such as health and homeowners insurance, property taxes, and other essential services have been unattended. At some point even math-adept individuals struggle with organizing and managing their financial affairs. Decreased acuity with such tasks also is an early sign of Alzheimer's disease. Cognitive shortcomings often tend to be a source of embarrassment, causing some elderly parents to deny assistance from loved ones, thus exacerbating the problem.

DISCOVERING RESIDENCY AND CARE OPTIONS

For some individuals, choosing to down-size their living space is a viable option. Selling the family home and purchasing a condo or apartment might be the answer, preferably with no stairs. Timing appears to be critical since many individuals have an emotional attachment to the family home. Safety and cost-effectiveness should be a higher, practical consideration. Stairs in the housing unit should be avoided because they become increasingly problematic as we age and experience decreased mobility, especially with hips and knees. In addition, consider social activity as well as nutritional issues when investigating living arrangements in your later years. Moving in with children or other family members may be an option but asking working children, who also are raising their own children, to care for you may only create more stress for everyone involved. All parties involved should carefully consider the effect of this housing decision.

Another viable option to investigate is a Continuing Care Retirement Community (CCRC).[41] CCRCs often offer multi-level living arrangements, including independent (or active) living, assisted-living, and skilled (nursing) facilities. If Medicaid assistance is a future possibility, look for facilities that accept residents receiving Medicaid assistance too. Keep in mind that moving into a new living arrangement in your later years, especially with impaired memory or cognitive issues, could be disorientating, further negatively impacting your emotional and psychological health. Thus, moving from a place to which you have become accustomed, whether from your home or from a care facility, to a new residence due to Medicaid needs could be disadvantageous, in turn causing a further decline in health. The objective is to find the most comfortable CCRC that allows you to live during your active years through hospice care, preferably before the onset of advanced cognitive impairment.

Carefully investigate options between and within such communities well in advance. CCRCs can have many different cost structures. Some residence agreements involve higher costs to join but limit long-term care costs in the future. Other agreements involve lower upfront costs but with no or limited future care options. Other facilities involve a payment back to the resident's estate upon his or her death, typically upon reoccupancy of the unit. Factors to consider when contemplating such housing, besides the financial ability to pay, are your age, anticipated longevity, future dementia possibilities, and health concerns. Other factors are social activity, desired amenities such as a pub, health center, chapel, and even the quality of the food served. Also investigate waiting lists for entry, which often are longer than anticipated.

Another matter to investigate is the ratings of the CCRC. Overall CCRC ratings involve both financial and healthcare facility regulations. Facilities that accept Medicare or Medicaid assistance, also must meet federal guidelines.[42] Regulatory mandates and oversight for healthcare facilities differ from state to state and must be reviewed carefully if you are considering facilities in different states.

KNOWING ALL ABOUT LONG-TERM CARE INSURANCE

LTC insurance is financial insurance. It protects you from having to deplete your life savings and, thus, enables you to keep your financial commitments to those you love. With LTC insurance, there is no one-size fits all solution. Applying for LTC insurance is like an à la carte menu whereby you choose a plan that you tailor to meet your expected needs. There are numerous considerations when deciding on a LTC insurance policy, and since purchasing LTC insurance is a decision you want to make once in your lifetime, you want to get it right the first time. In general, the motivation for pre-planning involves three major factors: 1) creating asset and income protection for spouse and family, 2) reducing the burden of care upon loved ones, and 3) achieving your personal preferences. Since you are applying for insurance, first you must be insurable. Thus, your health and overall insurability is a determining factor for its availability. After that, determining your personal goals for such coverage, family dynamics, living preferences, and available finances comes into play.

According to Armen Abrahamian,[43] a national LTC planner, "An often-critical question I ask clients when we initially meet is: without LTC protection, what assets would you first use for LTC when the time comes?" Although his clients may go to him for LTC insurance, other non-LTC insurance solutions may fit better given a client's objectives and needs. These options are life insurance and annuity-based LTC products or asset-transfer strategies when working with estate planning attorneys. Obtaining a LTC insurance policy shifts the financial burden to an insurance company, preserving family assets that otherwise would be used to pay for long-term care. For this purpose, it is important first to determine your need for care. In some cases, an all-encompassing Cadillac plan may be unnecessary. Perhaps a smaller daily or monthly amount of coverage is all you need to stave off complete depletion of family assets, which is especially important when considering a surviving spouse who may need financial resources. For some people, family support would cover home care needs and the type of coverage would be more for institutional care. Maybe a policy that covers the cost for some additional home care is all that is needed.

This leads to the next issue: How much of a burden could family members reasonably assume for your care? Often the burden falls upon women, such as the wife, daughter, or daughter-in-law in the family. But is she able to handle the LTC needs along with her own family, parenting, and work demands? Can she, as a member of the Sandwich Generation, adequately care for herself, her own household, her children (perhaps also saving for their college education), and her job responsibilities while simultaneously caring for a cognitively or physically impaired loved one?

Individuals caught in this Sandwich Generation tend to lose time at work and investment opportunities, thus their family commitment financially impacts their own future lives. The stress is palpable. Over time, the family caregiver's health becomes a factor that also must be considered.

In addition, consider that some women are not physically able to care for a larger impaired individual, thus putting her physical health at risk. A common occurrence with older women caring for a spouse or loved one is that since they tend to have brittle bones, one fall could cause a broken hip, hospitalization, and rehabilitation. Hospitals are a Petri dish of viruses, and many older patients catch pneumonia from their hospital stay, sometimes leading to their death. Given such a situation, who then would be the caregiver? If professional care were to be provided from a resource outside of the family, how would those costs be paid? According to Armen Abrahamian, "People don't understand just how exhausting it is to take care of a loved one until the illness occurs. Often the caregiver's health drastically declines, and they become just as ill as the patient. Burdens take on many forms: physical, psychological, financial and emotional." Given the strain on some family caregivers, sometimes critical decision-making is impaired when it is most needed.

Next, consider your personality type. Are you a planner, are you independent-minded, and do you expect to have more control over your life decisions? Would having a hired caregiver, perhaps from a different culture, living in your home or spending considerable time there, create more tension in your life? Is "remaining at home" a paramount factor for your LTC? Would living in a facility where meals are prepared for you and many social activities encouraged, be more to your taste? Depending upon your personality, and your expectations for, and reasonable availability of family support, involving family members in the LTC decision-making may be a critically important consideration.

As for LTC insurance policies, three basic types exist. A qualified LTC agent should be consulted to determine the best LTC strategy given your needs, objectives, and available financial resources.

1. **Traditional LTC:** The first type of LTC insurance is the traditional policy, which is the least expensive way to buy the largest amount of coverage. Policies provide a daily or monthly benefit to pay for home care, assisted living, and nursing facility care. Most policies have a lifetime cap, as well as options for inflation riders to help keep up with future rising LTC costs. Shared policies for couples also are available. According to Armen Abrahamian, "For some people a traditional plan makes more sense because it provides the best flexibility and value given the premiums paid." However, this type of insurance is like automobile or homeowner's insurance in that if

you do not need it, there is no benefit. In other words, you use it or lose it. In addition, rate increases in premiums may occur over time. Like all insurance coverage, actuaries constantly assess the profitability of insurance policies given changing demands and demographics. As a result, over the years, several LTC insurance companies have determined the need for rate increases for this type of LTC policy.

Some traditional LTC policies are offered as Partnership policies, which currently are available in forty-four states. In these states, a Partnership plan would enable an individual to protect assets above and beyond the state-mandated Medicaid asset limit (the maximum CSPA/CSRA) by the amount of LTC coverage paid out from the policy before applying for Medicaid coverage. For instance, if the Medicaid asset limit is $125,000 in your state and your spouse received $300,000 of LTC coverage under a Partnership plan, the spouse may keep $425,000 in assets and you will still qualify to receive Medicaid assistance without otherwise spending down assets to the $125,000 asset ceiling. See the next chapter for specifics on Medicaid spend-down planning issues.

2. **Hybrid and Chronic Illness Riders:** The second and third types of policies are cousins in that they both are built with life insurance policies at their base. These policies generally

fall into the category of either hybrid LTC policies or life insurance policies with LTC or chronic illness riders.

Hybrid LTC policies provide substantial LTC coverage while offering less life insurance benefits. LTC coverage is the emphasis. Governmental guidelines mandate a certain amount of life insurance coverage given the amount of LTC coverage for these policies. Payment may be made with either a single premium lump sum with no continuing payments, or be spread over a period of five years, ten years, or even a lifetime. These payments are guaranteed never to increase. For example, a sixty-year-old married female could pay a one-time lump sum of $100,000 for a hybrid LTC policy. Under the policy, she would be entitled to $382,000 in long-term care benefits. By the time she is eighty-five, her LTC benefits would have grown to more than $800,000. Should she never need LTC services, her beneficiaries would receive a death benefit of $118,000. In this example, if she changes her mind at any time, she would be entitled to a refund of $80,000. Given your finances and expected LTC needs, this type of plan may work best. For those with sizeable savings currently sitting in low interest accounts who mostly wish to self-insure, this is an excellent option. Another option is if such income is not needed for living expenses, you could allocate your required minimum distributions from qualified investments, such as an IRA or 401(k), to pay periodic LTC insurance premium payments.

The third type of LTC plan involves a life insurance policy with a LTC or chronic illness rider. Unlike the hybrid policy, which is designed to emphasize LTC coverage, this type of policy offers an equal amount of life insurance coverage and/or LTC coverage. For example, you may purchase a policy with a $300,000 death benefit. In the event you require long-term care, you may accelerate the death benefit, drawing down from the $300,000 of coverage to pay for care. In other words, unlike traditional life insurance, this plan provides a living benefit. If there is any remaining death benefit from this acceleration upon death, it is disbursed to your designated beneficiaries. In general, these policies are paid with ongoing premiums, most often over the individual's lifetime.

3. **Other Insurance Options:** The above-mentioned types of policies are the most popular LTC offerings today. Less popular are annuity products that can leverage the funds invested should a LTC illness occur. For those who currently have an annuity, especially with a low-cost basis, the Pension Protection Act enables clients to make a tax-free exchange into these annuity-based LTC policies and collect payments from them to pay LTC costs on a tax-favored basis. Often, the annuity

option is favorable when there are pre-existing medical issues.

Another alternative plan that may fit a person's needs is Short-Term Care Insurance (STCI). This is an expanding option throughout the country, now available in more than forty states. These plans have become increasingly popular because: 1) they are more affordable than LTC insurance; and 2) they are easier to qualify for, especially for those with pre-existing medical issues. They work similarly to LTC insurance; however, they generally provide coverage for just under one year, thus the name Short-Term Care Insurance. According to Armen Abrahamian, "Some clients are referred to me by estate planning lawyers and financial advisors for LTC insurance, yet often a combination of methods may work better after reviewing the client's individual situation. Sometimes they do not even need LTC insurance given the amount they have saved."[44] Armen recalls a creative example of fitting a strategy to a client's needs:

> For instance, consider Connie whose husband was experiencing a significant degree of health issues such that he likely would not have much longevity left. Preliminary underwriting for traditional LTC companies was not favorable. Available funds to pay for LTC were a bit limited. Ultimately, I crafted a plan

> whereby Connie purchased a short-term care policy that covers care at home, an assisted living facility, and a nursing home, with 300 days (10 months) of care at an initial daily benefit of $300. The figure will grow at a rate of 3% compounded annually. Her premium was just $126.50 per month. The plan provided some financial assistance for a short period of time in order to preserve the clients' investments for her.

Remember that when you need care, it takes income to pay for those services. As previously mentioned, an all-encompassing Cadillac plan may be unnecessary. For example, let us assume a single female with a monthly cost of care of $10,000. If her monthly income is $4,000 ($2,000 from Social Security and $2,000 from a pension), the $6,000 income gap could put a significant strain on her retirement assets. In addition to her care costs, she also needs to maintain her home, pay for food, pay her taxes, etc. Even owning a policy that would pay just $4,000 or $5,000 per month would remove much pressure from her retirement portfolio.

Whether to obtain LTC insurance is a personal decision given your needs, objectives, and finances. Regardless of the type, when a person owns insurance protection, he or she generally uses it, leading to a better life and better quality of care. This fact is one reason more affluent individuals tend to live longer. Consider that when you know you are covered by health insurance, you are more inclined to consult a doctor when you have health issues. Without the insurance, you know those high costs will come straight from your pocket, so you are inclined either to delay or not seek medical help. It is no different with LTC insurance.

The sweet spot to start planning and obtaining LTC insurance generally falls between ages 50-70, but more specifically ages 55-60. The earlier you start, the better, since that is when premiums are lower and you are generally in better health. Self-paying is an option too, either through adequate investments made throughout your life or obtaining a guaranteed income annuity with payments to you for life. A good financial planner or LTC specialist will compare all the strategies and options to find the best fit for you.

PREPAREDNESS QUESTIONS

1. Conduct an honest appraisal of your, or your loved one's, home living environment and the potential vulnerabilities that it poses in the elder years. What changes might you undertake to better prepare yourself or a loved one?

2. If you plan to stay at home as long as possible, list the people who could assist you around the home. Keep this list with your estate planning documents for family and care providers.

3. Depending upon your or you loved one's age, compile a list of nearby potential continuing care facilities that you or your loved one should consider for an alternate residence in your elder years or upon the onset of an End-Stage event. List your order of preference based on the pros and cons of each facility.

4. If living with family is a consideration, have you discussed this option with your family?

5. Are you of the age to consider LTC insurance, and if so, have you discussed this option with your financial planner or a LTC agent?

CHAPTER NINE:

QUALIFYING FOR MEDICAID

"Now read me the part again where I disinherit everybody."

— Peter Arno *New Yorker* cartoon showing a man in a suit speaking to his lawyer

For many people, understanding Medicaid, especially abruptly when in imminent need, is a harrowing experience. The Medicaid program, created by Title XIX of the 1965 Social Security Act, is extremely complicated, and the rules are applied differently in each state. For this reason, anyone with some semblance of wealth faced with the prospect of needing Medicaid assistance should consult a qualified estate planning or elder law attorney. The lawyer will analyze a couple's assets and determine what might be done given the laws of the state where they will apply for Medicaid assistance (where the applicant resides) to preserve that wealth for the non-applicant spouse. If the consultation is timely, the lawyer also may shelter wealth for other family members. Since Medicaid assistance is administered on the state level, it is impossible to provide a one-size-fits-all Medicaid plan of analysis. This chapter will explain general terminology and concepts regarding applying for Medicaid assistance. For consideration of a non-married person applying for Medicaid assistance, disregard the spousal provisions. Seek legal advice in your state of residence when considering Medicaid eligibility.

LEARNING TERMINOLOGY AND MEDICAID GUIDELINES

Traditionally, Medicaid assistance involved a person who went to an institution for LTC needs. Although home Medicaid assistance (known as a Medicaid Waiver) is widely available today, most of the terminology originally dealt with facility care, which will be the focus of this section to illustrate the program on an individual level. Home Medicaid Waiver programs have various state provisions, and appropriate legal advice is necessary to navigate eligibility for them.

Typically, a person seeking Medicaid assistance first has an event that requires advance care such as that provided in a hospital, nursing home, or Department of Veteran's Affairs (VA) facility, although veterans may have other options besides Medicaid to assist them, covered later in this chapter. For this reason, the Medicaid applicant is called the Institutional Spouse (IS), regardless of whether applying for institutional care or Medicaid Waiver coverage. The spouse not seeking assistance is referred to as the Community Spouse (CS), since he or she is generally living at home in the "community" and is not receiving Medicaid coverage. The date the IS first is medically eligible for institutional care is the "snapshot date." It is generally the date of institutionalization. Technically, the date is the first day of the month in which the IS accrued thirty continuous days in a facility. Note: If for some reason the IS stayed at a facility for fewer than thirty days, returned home, and then at some subsequent date reentered a facility thereafter requiring Medicaid assistance, the snapshot date would commence on the subsequent date of entering the facility.

To qualify for Medicaid assistance, the applicant (and the spouse, if married) must meet eligibility tests, which are: 1) being financially eligible; 2) having a medical need; and 3) being otherwise eligible; in other words, the applicant (and spouse, if married) must not have given away funds to meet financial eligibility. If the applicant (and spouse) do not meet these three tests, they will not be eligible for coverage. In addition, the IS must be a U.S. citizen or qualified non-citizen and reside in the state where applying for Medicaid coverage. For instance, a New York resident may not apply for Connecticut Medicaid assistance until he or she permanently resides in a Connecticut skilled Medicaid facility.

For the first financial eligibility test, the assets of both spouses are determined as of the snapshot date. Assets are classified as countable or non-countable. Non-countable assets are discussed in the next section of this chapter titled "Understanding Non-Countable Assets and Spend-Down." When Medicaid was initially instituted, states could choose to use a federally mandated "floor" for eligibility or a more restrictive means of eligibility (pursuant to section 209b of the Act). Initially, eleven states chose the more restrictive measures (known as 209b states); those states now number five. Accordingly, the other forty-five states follow Social Security Income (SSI) rules for Medicaid eligibility (informally known as SSI states); the other five follow slightly different rules. For the forty-five SSI states, Medicaid financial eligibility for an applicant is $2,000 in countable assets. The applicant may apply for Medicaid coverage with a greater sum of assets, but he or she will not be eligible until possessing $2,000 or less. In 209b states, a countable asset threshold of $1,600 is required to be eligible. If married, the spouse's assets also are a factor because the couple is considered "one unit" for Medicaid eligibility. If both spouses require Medicaid assistance, the asset eligibility threshold applies to each of them and is thus multiplied by two. For instance, if in an SSI state, to be eligible, they together must have $4,000 or less in assets.

If only one spouse requires care, the government does not want the CS to be impoverished. Accordingly, the CS must have assets (as of the snapshot date) within a maximum and minimum state-determined amount established to provide the CS with enough assets to live without becoming impoverished (in the state's opinion and rarely enough in the CS's opinion). The maximum and minimum amounts are called the maximum and minimum community spousal protected allowance (CSPA). In some states, such as in Massachusetts, it is called the community spousal resource allowance (CSRA). This allowance amount is state specific. Even within the SSI or 209b states, the minimum and maximum CSPA/CSRA differs. If the couple has more than this amount, they are ineligible for care until they spend down their assets to within the applicable threshold amount. Some states divide the assets as of the snapshot date and force spouses to spend-down any excess assets over the CS and IS's requisite maximum amounts. Other states allow the IS's excess assets to pass to the CS up to his or her maximum CSPA or CSRA amount.

Remember, if a couple has exhausted the benefits of a LTC insurance policy and that policy qualified as a Partnership Plan, the funds exhausted under the LTC policy are added to the maximum CSPA that the CS may keep. For example, if the LTC policy provided $300,000 of care, the CS may keep $300,000 in assets in addition to the maximum CSPA.

UNDERSTANDING NON-COUNTABLE ASSETS AND SPEND-DOWN

What if a couple has excess countable assets to qualify? The couple then must engage in a careful spend-down of their assets. To do so, the couple must determine what assets are non-countable, or how to change legally the title of an asset to make it a non-countable asset. First, personal property and household items are non-countable. Second, the home (not an investment property or second home) is a non-countable asset, but the IS may not be its owner. A deed may be recorded in the appropriate Registry of Deeds in your town or county before filing the Medicaid application to transfer title solely into the CS's name. The home, therefore, may be conveyed (retitled) solely in the CS's name, regardless of the look-back period. A cap exists on the equity of the home; however, the amount depends upon the state of residency. This equity cap was established in 2006 at $500,000 in some states and $750,000 in others. This equity cap is adjusted annually. The CS also may own one vehicle, and in certain instances, the IS may own a vehicle if it is for his or her special needs.

Third, the death benefit of life insurance policies, other than the cash value of any permanent policies, is non-countable. Fourth, the couple's burial plot is non-countable. The couple may also enter into a burial contract for such expenses. Last, since the CS's vehicle and home are non-countable assets and considering the limited amount of the applicable CSPA on which the CS must learn to live, any further excess countable assets may be used to provide needed repairs and upkeep to the home. This work generally entails updating or replacing material elements of the home such as the roof, furnace, water heater, kitchen, or bathroom. The CS also may trade-in the CS's existing vehicle for a newer or more reliable one.

Some states allow for other spend-down measures such as funding certain annuities. Again, be cautioned: Some bank representatives and financial planners, unknowledgeable about Medicaid guidelines, may erroneously advise annuities that are not acceptable as non-countable assets. Since many annuities are non-terminable, meaning their owner may be unable to terminate or alter the annuity, their ownership creates a difficult disqualifying event for Medicaid eligibility. If Medicaid assistance might be in your foreseeable future, especially within the next five years, seek legal assistance before investing in an annuity. They are not all the same!

Further exceptions allow permissible transfers under the Medicaid guidelines, such as a child-caregiver living in the home and providing care to the IS for at least two years prior to his or her applying for Medicaid assistance. To qualify for this exception, along with the Medicaid application, there must be a written statement from the IS's treating physician stating that the IS otherwise would have needed assistance, but for the child caregiver's assistance. In such case, the home may be transferred to the child-caregiver, regardless of the look-back period. For this reason, if you are a child caregiver, it likewise would behoove you to be involved with the IS's doctor and other medical visits. Another exception allows a couple to transfer any assets to a disabled or blind child (determined pursuant to Social Security Income eligibility criteria). Again, this exception is not subject to the look-back period.

Of course, Medicaid planning measures exist to shelter assets if properly pursued prior to the five-year look-back period. Permissive options vary by state, but in some states, you also could make transfers to a properly drafted irrevocable income-only or fully discretionary trust. However, in some states, such as Connecticut, the state may view the percentage of trust income allowed to be distributed from the trust to the couple, including that percentage of the trust corpus, as countable assets, thus defeating the trust's main purpose. Such trusts are irrevocable, and neither the IS or CS may be trustees, so you will be able to control neither the trust's assets nor the distribution of its principal. For discretionary trusts, you have no guarantee that income or principal of the trust would be distributed to you since trust distributions are at the sole discretion of the independent trustee. In addition, if you require Medicaid assistance within five years from transferring assets to either trust, the transfer would be a disqualifying event. Another factor to consider is that lawyers may not assist in impoverishing a client for the purpose of a client's qualifying for Medicaid benefits. Thus, the timing for such planning is critical.

The second test is medical eligibility. When a person applies for Medicaid coverage, it must be proven to the state that he or she is "medically needy for care," known as Medicaid Eligibility. To qualify for institutional Medicaid coverage, the applicant must need assistance with at least 2-3 Activities of Daily Living (ADL). If the applicant has dementia or cognitive impairments, even though he or she does not require assistance with ADLs, but requires prompting or assistance to complete such tasks, the IS nevertheless will qualify for Medicaid assistance.

The third test is that the applicant must be otherwise eligible. Besides considering the allowable assets as of the snapshot date, the couple must report all accounts, income, expenses, and transfers of assets within the five years prior to the snapshot date—the five-year look-back period. All such items must be accounted for in the Medicaid application. Otherwise, people may transfer their assets and immediately apply for Medicaid assistance. Be careful; gifts made pursuant to the annual exclusion under the IRC §121 ($15,000 per person per year for year 2020) are *not* permissible transfers under Medicaid guidelines. Any "transfer" of one or more assets for less than full value within this look-back period is an improper transfer under the guidelines, regardless of the annual exclusion. Many advisors such as accountants, financial planners, and lawyers not knowledgeable with Medicaid guidelines could provide disastrous gifting advice that, if made during the look-back period, will make the IS ineligible for Medicaid assistance when needed. Thus, it is critical not only to seek advice from a lawyer knowledgeable with Medicaid guidelines, but to seek this advice well in advance of a potential event requiring Medicaid assistance.

What if an ineligible transfer were made during the look-back period? States have a penalty divisor, which is the average monthly cost of care in that state, to determine the number of months the IS is ineligible for Medicaid assistance due to the improper transfer. The value of the assets transferred (for less than adequate consideration, or the "gift" amount) is divided by the penalty divisor to determine the number of months of ineligibility. For example, if the penalty divisor is $10,000 and the value of the ineligible transfer is $20,000, the IS will be ineligible for two months from the date he or she would otherwise be eligible. For asset threshold purposes, eligibility is the first day of the month the couple qualified for Medicaid assistance under the guidelines, which if managed properly, is the month the Medicaid application is filed. Therefore, assume further that but for the prior $20,000 gift (or gifts), the couple qualified for Medicaid assistance when they filed. In such an example, the couple would be penalized two months after the month they filed and would have to use their non-countable assets to cover the LTC costs during this ineligibility period. Consider further the monthly costs of LTC (in Chapter Five) that apply in your state. Can the recipients of the "gift" return it to avoid the ineligibility period? Sure. Or, another option would be for the recipients, usually family members, to pay for the care during the ineligibility period. But this option only makes sense if the monthly cost of care is less than the monthly penalty divisor, which in most cases, it will not be.

What if a child who received such transfer provided care for the IS? Could the child argue that the gifts are payment for the provided services? Perhaps. However, states tend to consider any assistance by family, in absence of a written contract, to be for love and affection and disallow the "payments" (transfers in Medicaid parlance) pursuant to an oral agreement. What would such a written agreement be called? A Care Agreement, which would delineate the parties to the contract, the payments, and the services to be provided. For a valid contract, there must be a "bargained for exchange"; in other words, fees for services as described in the written agreement. Best practice dictates having a lawyer who is knowledgeable with the Medicaid guidelines and typical fees for delineated care in the state in which you reside, to draft the agreement. Such planning optimally should be well in advance of potential need for Medicaid assistance. Also, keep in mind someone other than a lawyer who drafts a contract and provides legal advice may be subject to a claim of the unauthorized practice of law. Does this law preclude the family from drafting and executing such an agreement? No, but remember the adage: "He who represents himself has a fool for a client." Seek appropriate advice.

Once an IS qualifies for Medicaid assistance, is the income of the CS and/or IS considered? For a Medicaid Waiver applicant, the asset threshold is not the only concern. A permissible income amount exists based upon a formula set by federal Medicaid guidelines. Income never is a concern for an applicant (and spouse) for institutional assistance because: 1) the spouse's income does not count toward a Medicaid applicant, and 2) if seeking institutional coverage, all the income is paid to the facility as the co-pay amount except for the personal maintenance needs allowance and the individual's actual medical insurance costs.

The monthly maintenance needs allowance (MMNA) is the minimum income amount the CS may retain to avoid impoverishment. It is tied to U.S. poverty levels, which are annually updated. The MMNA may be augmented with extra demonstrated expenses, subject to approval. In addition, the IS's income may be diverted to the CS to increase the CS's MMNA up to the applicable maximum MMNA cap. The CS also has other allowances such as for shelter, utilities, and personal needs. Each state provides its own tailored MMNA and other allowance amounts. Any excess income goes to the facility for cost of care. Medicaid then pays the remaining balance of the full cost of care. What if the CS requires more than the allowed assets or income? Then the CS could ask for more when applying, and if the Medicaid application is denied, the CS could ask for a hearing to argue his or her case for more assistance.

AVOIDING STATE REIMBURSEMENT UPON DEATH OF SPOUSE

The Medicaid analysis does not only require eligibility considerations. You also must consider state reimbursement for Medicaid benefits when the IS dies. Upon the IS's subsequent death, the state will place a lien on the IS's probate assets for reimbursement of provided Medicaid funds. Normally, the IS only would have assets no greater than the allowed $2,000 (or $1,600 for 209b states) amount. But what if the CS dies first and has a simple "I love you" will that gives all the CS's assets to the IS? In such a case, the State would have a lien on the IS's inheritance up to the Medicaid assistance amount provided to the IS. If, after repayment of the Medicaid lien, the IS owns assets greater in value than the $2,000 asset threshold, Medicaid assistance will cease until such assets are spent down—typically on the IS's care—until the IS's assets are within the $2,000 asset threshold. For this reason, seeking guidance from a knowledgeable estate or elder planning attorney to review and change the CS's will is an essential part of Medicaid planning. Otherwise, the CS's assets are protected and not subject to state seizure.

DISCOVERING OPTIONS FOR VETERANS

The motto of the U.S. Department of Veterans Affairs (VA), as stated by Abraham Lincoln on March 4, 1865, is:

> With malice toward none, with charity for all, with firmness in the right as God gives us to see the right, let us strive on to finish the work we are in, to bind up the nation's wounds, *to care for him who shall have borne the battle and for his widow, and his orphan,* to do all which may achieve and cherish a just and lasting peace among ourselves and with all nations. [Emphasis mine.]

Among other benefits, such as the GI Bill and medical and VA healthcare, veterans may qualify for post-service payments due to injuries during war time ("Compensation"), and VA pensions ("Pensions"). Veterans may be awarded compensation if they prove there is some nexus or relationship to a permanent physical disability or injury during a service-related activity during the nation's time of war. A veteran cannot receive both compensation and a pension, only the higher benefit of the two. The surviving spouse of a qualifying veteran who died from a service-related injury may collect a lifetime income stream known as "Dependency and Indemnity Compensation." Veterans with low income may qualify for a pension for medical assistance such as home-care/aid and attendance/hospitalization. Note that all veterans over the age of sixty-five are presumed disabled.

There is an asset limit, as with Medicaid, to qualify for such benefits. As of October 2018, a veteran (and spouse) may have no more than $129,000 annually in countable assets. According to Matthew Stillman,[45] an estate planning and elder law attorney with an LL.M. degree, an accredited VA counselor, and former President of Connecticut's NAELA:

> This number, however, is a bit of a misnomer because the couple's annual income is annualized and "added" to their countable asset total to constitute that amount. So, for instance, a couple with $80,000 of assets may qualify if their annual income is less than $50,000. A couple with income of $60,000 ($5,000/month) must have less than $70,000 of assets to qualify. Additionally, to qualify for Veterans' benefits, one must have qualifying medical expenses that generally meet or exceed their incomes. Expenses for items such as residential fees, taxes, cars, insurance, food,

> rent, and utilities, do not come into consideration—only Medicaid expenses. If one's medical expenses (caregivers, co-pays, supplies, insurance, etc.) all equal or exceed the veteran's (and spouse's) income, they may qualify for additional VA Pension and Aid & Attendance benefits if they meet the other qualifying tests.

The veteran does not have to be in the theater of combat; only to have served ninety days during wartime (defined by statute) and have medical need. Medical need is defined as demonstrated need for care (from a doctor), or the veteran is in a "Protective Residence," such as a senior facility or assisted living center. In addition, if dishonorably discharged, the veteran is not eligible for such benefits. To determine if you or your spouse may qualify, consult an accredited VA attorney, VSO, or Veteran administration staff for assistance. Pursuant to 38 U.S.C. §5904 and §5905, such assistance must be free for the application and first appeal if denied.

For some veterans in need of long-term care, more than 100 Community Living Centers (CLC) or VA Nursing Homes across the country may be available without needing to apply for Medicaid. Attorney Stillman also advises:

In states like Connecticut where there are not any/sufficient nursing homes available for veterans, if a veteran has a qualifying Medical disability (70% compensation rating or better), there are a series of nursing homes that allow a veteran to be admitted at no cost, and the VA pays the entire bill; no Medicaid is needed. This only occurs in some states and if the veteran has a 70% service-connected disability rating or better.

ELLEN'S CASE

After Ellen's initial meeting with her lawyer, the issues confronting her must be analyzed and prioritized. The most immediate concern is how long Bob will likely be in a rehabilitation facility and how much of this time Medicare will cover the costs. Any time not covered by Medicare Ellen must self-pay since she and Bob do not have long-term care insurance. We then must determine if Bob can feasibly return home after his rehabilitation, and, if so, how much it would cost to make required repairs for him to do so. A home assessment will be made to determine what is needed for the home to be safe given Bob's new status. More than likely, a ramp must be installed to enter their home, hand bars and railings will be needed in the downstairs bathroom, and the downstairs living room will need to be made into Bob's new bedroom since he cannot safely navigate stairs. Ellen will have to obtain estimates from carpenters for the work needed. She may not be able to care for Bob solely. If Ellen cannot safely assist Bob with his ambulatory issues—moving from bed to bathroom to living quarters—she may need to hire caregivers too. If Bob requires 24/7 care, perhaps another room may have to be prepared as a bedroom for a caregiver. In the state where Bob and Ellen live, caregivers could cost $4,000-$6,500 a month, probably closer to the higher figures since Bob likely will need assistance with medications and, thus, need an RN to visit.

If Ellen chooses the home option, given the costs and the value of their investments, in less than three years, their funds will be exhausted and they must look to Medicaid for assistance. The unknown factors are how Bob's condition might deteriorate and if he will require facility care, even after the expenses for repairs. The other qualitative factor is the continued stress on Ellen for taking care of Bob at home. At this time, she may not be mentally and emotionally able to accept this eventuality.

To adequately prepare for potential Medicaid assistance, she first must retrieve and organize all assets she and Bob own and provide statements of their values as of the date Bob entered the hospital—the snapshot date. Then, she must collect statements for the last five years of each asset/account. If an account were closed or opened during this period, it must be explained.

Second, she must account for all present living expenses, those during the five-year period, and a determination of future needs, especially to determine her present health and home expenses. Any unaccounted expenses must be explained. Third, if she pursues Medicaid Waiver (home care) assistance, all sources of income from both Bob and Ellen should be determined to analyze eligibility given her state's guidelines. If facility care becomes an option, these figures will be needed to determine how much income Ellen may keep, given her expenses. The lawyer will analyze and present the options to Ellen and assist her with choosing the best course of action, costs, and timing for action. Moreover, the lawyer's staff or a care provider may help Ellen with most of these endeavors.

As part of the Medicaid analysis, the lawyer will draft a deed to be executed and recorded in the appropriate Registry of Deeds to put the title of the home solely in Ellen's name. If Bob had executed a financial power of attorney that authorizes Ellen to transfer real estate for him, she, as his appointed attorney-in-fact under the power of attorney, could sign the deed for him. However, since she did not execute one, she first must file a guardianship/conservatorship action in probate court for the court to grant her authority to transfer Bob's title in the home. Once completed, the home then will be a non-countable asset. Next, the lawyer will review Ellen's will and, if necessary, amend it (via a codicil) or draft a new one so that it does not gift assets in her name to Bob if she dies before him. In some states, if Ellen dies first, regardless of her will (or codicil), the state will claim Ellen's probate assets up to that state's forced, or statutory, spousal share. The remaining assets will pass to her other heirs pursuant to the will.

Then, the lawyer must determine the total amount of assets Ellen may keep—the maximum CSPA—after Bob's $2,000 allowable cap. If assets remain over this maximum CSPA amount, a plan must be created to spend down the excess assets. Since it is highly probable that Bob will require Medicaid assistance within the next five years (the look-back), transferring assets to an income-only or discretionary trust is not an option. For these excess assets that she must spend down, Ellen must determine how to spend them permissively within Medicaid guidelines. She could choose to purchase a new car, make repairs and improvements to the home, acquire medical equipment for Bob, or perhaps obtain a special Medicaid-approved annuity. This annuity must be irrevocable, non-assignable, actuarially sound, and provide equal fixed payments to Ellen throughout its term. The state department administering Medicaid services must be a named remainder beneficiary in case she dies before the term expires.

To be actuarially sound, the annuity must pay out within Ellen's life expectancy according to the life expectancy table from the Social Security Administration. In other words, after rounding

Ellen's age to the nearest six months at the time of applying—let us assume the age is seventy-nine—her life expectancy according to its calculation is just over ten years. Therefore, an annuity with a term of ten years or less would be actuarially sound. The terms of the annuity may not allow it to be transferred to anyone; it may not be canceled or cashed out, and it must provide fixed payments to Ellen for the chosen annuity term. If Ellen dies within the term, the state will receive the remaining annuity amount up to the Medicaid assistance provided to Bob. If Ellen lives past the annuity term, all the payments are hers to handle as she wishes.

After reviewing all Medicaid issues for Bob's application, Ellen's future needs must be considered. She must consider if she should continue to live in their existing home if Bob moves to a facility. Would downsizing her housing, hopefully with less costs, make more sense? Would going to a CCRC facility make sense?

It is an incredibly daunting and emotionally draining effort to handle these issues when a spouse has suddenly befallen a life-altering event. Ellen may have to push herself beyond her comfort zone and beyond mental, and quite possibly, physical exhaustion. It may be difficult for her to know if she will make the best decisions for her and Bob. It is a suddenly scary time in her life, especially since she has not been educated or prepared for it. Then comes the legal bill.

PREPAREDNESS QUESTIONS

1. Have you, or will you based upon your budget, have enough savings either to self-pay or insure for your and your spouse's LTC needs?

2. If you are a U.S. Veteran, determine whether you served during time of war and whether you qualify for Veteran benefits. Find a VA counselor if you require help.

3. If you, a spouse, or a loved one might require Medicaid assistance, find a qualified estate planning and elder lawyer for a consultation and possible estate planning changes well before the need arises.

CHAPTER TEN:

PROTECTING YOUR FAMILY: SQUABBLES AND DEATH

"Death is not the end. There remains the litigation over the estate."
— Leo Tolstoy, *Anna Karenina*

The decline and ultimate passing of a family member often shifts the family's balance of power, sometimes resulting in the expression of formerly hidden, yet disruptive tendencies. These childhood-rooted intricacies previously held in check in times of a parent's good health may, upon that parent's weakness, create, in turn, family disharmony, conflict, and their ensuing legal costs. The more brutally honest that parents are about their children when they design their estate plan with their estate planning lawyer, the better the lawyer may guide them toward an appropriate estate plan that handles such potential family issues. Examples of troubling family dynamics with children are their personal insecurities, attitudes, and acumen with money; competitiveness with each other; jealousy of siblings (or their spouses); spousal influences; lifestyle choices and personal judgments; occupational status; sense of entitlement; substance abuse, etc. Hoping that the kids will work it all out may not be the best family plan. A review of famous people, from BB King and James Brown to oil tycoon J. Howard Marshall II and Anna Nicole Smith, illustrates this point. Acknowledging and managing these dynamics, then carefully creating an appropriate estate plan while also appointing the best individual(s) for your financial, health, executor, and trustee duties, may greatly reduce the likelihood of ensuing lawsuits, which add costs and more family disunity. This chapter reviews shifting family dynamics when a matriarch or patriarch experiences declining health and dies, along with ways to avoid negative family issues by creating a well-considered estate plan.

LEARNING FAMILY ISSUES IN DECLINING HEALTH

During the decline in health of a parent, absent children may believe the child-caregiver receives a greater share of that parent's attention and money—whether given or stolen—disregarding the sacrifices that the child-caregiver makes to care for the parent. Sometimes, the accusations are warranted. Children less capable of self-sufficiency may prey upon a weakened parent. Abuses may occur. For example, consider a father with Parkinson's disease who lived in the Northeast; his troubled daughter and her boyfriend moved into dad's home, which was in a rather affluent neighborhood. The only other child lived out of state, managing his family and career. The father's neighbors, noticing not only the daughter's sudden presence in her father's life but also numerous moving trucks with Florida license plates sporadically at the property, contacted state officials to investigate. The officials eventually found the father relegated to the basement of the home during the winter, sleeping on a cot full of his feces with only a wool blanket for warmth. By the time the matter came before a probate judge and a lawyer was appointed as conservator to investigate, the father's belongings, money, and daughter were long gone. When the father died soon afterwards, the only inheritance the out-of-state son received was the funeral home bill.

Legal actions are available to remedy abuse; however, often the burden of proof upon the accuser and the cost to pursue such actions are steep. Other times, the person preying on the elderly parent is judgment-proof, having expended all stolen property to his or her negative habits. (See Chapter Seven: Spotting Financial Elder Abuse for more information on this subject.) Since this book is about educating and empowering you to avoid risk, what then can be done to avoid, or at least minimize, these concerns? In short, plan to avoid them.

Probate courts provide guardianship/conservatorship actions in which a person is appointed to manage the health and financial matters of someone at risk, with court accountability and oversight. There is a cost, but perhaps it is minimal given the potentially harmful family dynamics. However, discussing the matter with an estate planning lawyer in advance of declining health may avoid these negative issues and at a fraction of the cost. The lawyer could create a healthcare directive and financial power of attorney to appoint the appropriate people for the tasks involved. Executing these documents assumes the elder has the requisite capacity to sign them. Also, appointing someone merely because he or she is a child may provide authority to that child to abuse or overreach. Perhaps appointing a professional solely or jointly with a child would make better sense. Professionals must, and should know how to, be accountable for their health and financial decisions under such documents, often with higher legal accountability given their professional status. Likewise, if a family member is appointed to handle such tasks, it is advisable for that person to maintain a log to account for his or her actions, and when in doubt, to consult an estate or elder planning attorney to determine the best course of action. These procedures may be useful if an accuser of abuse meets his or her burden of proving "irregularities" sufficient for a judge to order the appointed child to account for his or her activities. State courts, either on the trial level, probate courts, or both, have authority to hear a cause of action for misuse of funds by an agent appointed under a power of attorney both before and after the principal dies. Likewise, for accusations of trustee abuse, trust beneficiaries may sue the trustee for breach of fiduciary duty, misuse of trust funds, or pursue other available legal actions.

Another option for financial matters would be to create a trust, fund it by transferring assets into it, and appoint the appropriate trustee(s) to manage the trust assets. Again, simply appointing a child may not be the best choice, practically or even according to the IRS Code, depending upon the distribution clauses in the trust. Although states are improving elder abuse prevention, from mandatory reporters to legislation that creates criminal offenses for elder abuse, it still might be a better fit in certain circumstances to consider a professional or trust company as a trustee. Consulting and hiring care providers also may be appropriate, not only to avoid potential negative family dynamics but also to alleviate the family burden and added stress of care for a declining parent. Lastly, consider a Continuing Care Community or similar facility that will have numerous individuals there to assist, especially as the need for care increases when End-Stage issues progress. Ultimately, assess and plan your life to avoid these potential issues.

After suffering a heart attack and changing his residence to a facility after rehabilitation, a man contacted his lawyer to discuss his daughter's taking, without his knowledge, more than

$100,000 of his funds and gambling it away at the local casino. She was the client's appointed attorney-in-fact under his power of attorney. His trust provided that each of his two children would receive an equal share of his estate, but after the costs of his rehabilitation and living costs (in addition to his home housing costs), his estate was worth far less than anticipated. He was hurt and emotional about the issue, and he wanted to be fair to his son.

The lawyer explained that he should terminate the existing power of attorney, notify all of his financial institutions of the termination, and execute another one appointing his son. Next, the lawyer explained the probate process and its potential costs to make the daughter account for the misappropriation of his funds. Ultimately, although distraught, the man agreed to eliminate her as a trust beneficiary since in his words, "Well, I now know what she did with her inheritance." Within days, the lawyer visited the man with a power of attorney termination, a new power of attorney, and a trust amendment. After signing, the client was sad, but he was relieved that the issue could be resolved. In addition, his lawyer advised him to write a letter in his own words about why he had made this change and to send copies to his successor trustees. After the man subsequently died, the daughter had no recourse to contest her father's will since all his assets were held in trust, and she wisely chose not to file a costly action in the trial court for an inheritance.

LEARNING FAMILY ISSUES UPON DEATH

What are some family issues to prevent after death? Consider again the previously mentioned potential shift in the family balance when a parent falters. Also, consider who is the appointed executor of the will or the trustee of the trust of the deceased parent. How will the other family members handle this person's authority and control over estate assets during the slow and long probate administration or trust management period? Will there be family harmony and trust, or disunity as the appointed person performs his or her duties? Handling the transfer of assets in probate court involves court oversight. It also involves many tasks, which may not be suited for certain individuals, especially given the existence of negative family dynamics. Sometimes, simply choosing a family member as fiduciary, either in your will or trust, may only exacerbate family issues. Other times, gifting wealth upon death outright to family heirs is the worst estate plan.

1. **Probate Administration and Avoidance:** Probate procedures vary by state with different applicable probate administration processes depending upon the type and amount of probate assets. Typically, the first step in the probate administration of a decedent involves admitting the will and having the executor (a fiduciary) appointed to administer the probate estate. Interested parties and heirs at law may contest the validity of the will or the appointment of the executor, adding

more time and expense to the administration process, not to mention the aforementioned family disunity. If the decedent died intestate—had no will—state statutes handle the distribution of the decedent's assets with a one-size-fits-all statutory procedure.

Although the probate administration process of a decedent's estate varies by state, in general, once appointed, the executor must: 1) "marshal" assets—title probate assets into his or her name as the fiduciary; 2) present an inventory of the assets and their date-of-death values to the probate court; 3) determine the validity of creditor claims for debts of the decedent and determine whether to pay or disclaim them; 4) handle lawsuits brought by creditors for payment of debts; 5) pursue lawsuits brought by the decedent against others or institute lawsuits on the decedent's behalf; 6) account for all items of income and expense during the administration period; 7) present an accounting or financial report to the court; 8) manage and file an estate tax form; and 9) file the decedent's income taxes for year of death; and 10) distribute the probate assets according to court direction. The formality of some of these roles varies depending upon the probate court's jurisdiction. In addition, the executor may have to bring or defend legal challenges regarding the proper interpretation of a will clause, especially if one is not well written. Further issues deal with the management of estate assets during the administration period. Examples of such issues might be whether to sell estate assets, such as stocks or real estate, or merely transfer such assets outright (called "in-kind") to the appropriate estate beneficiaries as provided in the decedent's will. Other tasks are assessing capital gain/loss and income taxes of the decedent and those of the estate (or the beneficiaries depending upon how these assets are handled). It is a thankless job, especially for a family member not otherwise experienced with probate administration matters or who already has a busy private and work life. An estate planner usually is quite useful for navigating through the administration process maze.

With a well-constructed estate plan, assets could be titled to avoid this complicated and lengthy probate process, as discussed at more length in Chapters Three and Six. For example, assets with designated beneficiaries, such as life insurance or qualified retirement accounts, pass outside of probate, although the executor will have to contact these institutions and have assets distributed to the designated beneficiaries. Assets held in trust not only are not subject to public view but also avoid the probate process. In this case, the trustee would handle how to hold, manage, and distribute the income and principal of the trust assets, according to the trust's terms. The trustee, too, must assess capital gain/loss and income taxes associated with trust assets, but the public, and often a lengthy probate administration process, is avoided.

2. **Issues with Inheriting:** Next, consider how the beneficiaries will handle this influx of wealth. In the case of all assets passing outright to a spouse, can he or she effectively manage the assets? Will there be tension if a surviving spouse receives all assets outright, especially a spouse who is not the parent of the decedent's surviving children? Should the spouse receive such wealth in hand, especially if he or she has special needs or is likely to apply for Medicaid assistance? If you appoint your spouse as executor or trustee, will you create family acrimony if he or she is not also the parent of some of your children? The ability of a spouse, child, or other beneficiary is always a drafting consideration. Another consideration is whether your estate plan provides a disproportionate amount to each child, perhaps to account for extra lifetime gifts to a child or for other reasons. This plan may increase the likelihood of family issues that lead to litigation.

When creating your estate plan, consider the likely amount of wealth transfer upon your death, each beneficiary's ability to handle the wealth he or she receives, and whether it is best to gift the beneficiary's inheritance outright or to hold the assets in trust for their benefit under terms you determine.

In the case of assets passing to children, how will they handle such newfound wealth? Are they too young? Too inexperienced or irresponsible with money? At high risk of lawsuits or divorce? Again, a thorough and honest discussion with an estate planning attorney is key to the construction of a solid plan. Assets held in trust, properly drafted, will shield wealth from a beneficiary's creditors, yet still provide financial assistance to that beneficiary. (See estate planning discussions in Chapters Three and Six.) One example of protecting assets is when choosing a beneficiary with special needs. In such a case, consider holding assets for his or her benefit in a specifically designed special needs trust. Otherwise, an outright inheritance to the beneficiary may affect his or her qualifications to receive public assistance. Likewise, if the special needs beneficiary has received public assistance, the state may seize the inheritance for reimbursement of such provided aid. (See explanation in Chapter Three.)

Medicaid also has an impact upon your estate plan. If a decedent's surviving spouse has received Medicaid assistance, upon the decedent's death, the state agency administering the program will demand reimbursement from the decedent's spouse's estate for provided Medicaid assistance to the surviving spouse. If there are remaining assets passing to the surviving spouse after this repayment that would otherwise disqualify the spouse from receiving Medicaid assistance, such assistance will be denied until the surviving spouse spends down below the allowable Medicaid asset level of $2,000, or $1,600, depending upon the state. If Medicaid is a future possibility for the surviving spouse, such wealth likewise will have to be spent down for that spouse to qualify for Medicaid benefits. This may be desirable. However, alternate estate plans exist to minimize or prevent such spend down. A good estate or elder lawyer could carefully plan for such a situation. In some states, a plan would be to change the will of a Medicaid applicant's spouse, so that if he or she passes first, only the statutory spousal share goes to the surviving (Medicaid-recipient) spouse. All other assets could pass to family members and beneficiaries as the testator desires. As mentioned previously, in some states an income-only trust or a discretionary trust would be a viable plan. State and federal laws apply, and they are specific to each state and generally complicated; therefore, seek appropriate guidance.

Lastly, as of the year 2020, beneficiaries of qualified retirement plans other than a spouse or a disabled or minor child may no longer choose the beneficiary's life expectancy for the payout term for such inherited retirement plans. A surviving spouse may use his or her life expectancy for the payout period, with some exceptions. But as of the year 2020, for non-spousal, abled-body, or adult beneficiaries, the payout is a mandated ten-year term. If the beneficiary is a minor or disabled, once he or she no longer is disabled or a minor, the ten-year term commences. Why is this important? Because prior to 2020, a parent could protect more vulnerable children when they inherited such assets by holding the assets in trust for the child's benefit upon the parent's death and stretch the term for holding the retirement funds according to the child's life expectancy. This term usually is much longer than the deceased parent's life expectancy and the new ten-year period. Before, the wealth would trickle out at a slower pace and over a longer duration of time to protect the beneficiary. In most plans, the income taxes due on the distributions would be at the beneficiary's marginal income tax rate too. Now, the assets held in such plans must distribute to such beneficiaries at greater amounts, over a shorter period, which in turn accelerates the income taxes upon the trust distributions. The concept behind this "wind down" process is the federal mandatory required minimum distributions (RMDs) that a plan holder must withdraw at age seventy-two, or in the case of an inherited retirement plan, the ten-year term. With a longer term, the RMDs were lower. Since the plan distributions allowed for lower RMDs, it meant less income taxes due and a greater period of protection to the beneficiary.

One still may plan for a trust to hold qualified retirement accounts. The trust may dictate that the trustee distribute such accounts to the beneficiary within the ten-year term or accumulate the RMDs in trust. The first arrangement is considered a conduit trust provision, such that when the RMDs are withdrawn, they pass through the trust out to the beneficiary. Under the new law, RMDs now do not have to be withdrawn throughout the ten-year term. The entire amount may be withdrawn in the tenth year. Through using the conduit trust provision for retirement accounts, the income taxes generated from the withdrawals could be distributed out to the beneficiary for him or her to report, and pay, on his or her income tax return. The alternative is to allow the trustee to hold the RMDs in trust, longer than the ten-year term. However, this option subjects the trust, not its beneficiaries, to the income tax on the RMDs. Trusts, in turn, are subject to the highest marginal income tax rate, which is generally higher than that of the beneficiary. Again, the key is to be educated and to plan given the family situation.

PREPAREDNESS QUESTIONS

1. Honestly assess your family dynamics and the personalities of your family members, especially how they may change with your illness or death. What is your plan to avoid any potential risk of family disharmony?

2. Review again the people you appoint in your estate plan and determine if they are the best people to choose given any foreseen issues with Question 1 above.

3. Are you the likely caregiver for a parent, uncle, or aunt? If so, what precautions are you prepared to take to protect yourself?

4. Honestly determine how well each of your beneficiaries will manage his or her inheritance from you.

CHAPTER ELEVEN:

SEEING MEDICAID FROM THE FEDERAL AND STATE FOCUS

"Loyalty to the Nation all the time, loyalty to the Government when it deserves it."

— Mark Twain

Medicaid is a joint federal and state program created in the United States by Title XIX of the 1965 Social Security Act, which, after Medicare, is "the largest health program as measured by expenditures."[46] The federal and state governments share Medicaid costs, which are increasing. The Centers for Medicare & Medicaid Services (CMS) is the federal agency that administers Medicaid for the federal government. Beginning in 2014, with the passage of the Affordable Care Act, states were allowed to expand coverage to non-elderly adults with incomes up to 138 percent of the federal poverty level.[47] All states (and five U.S. territories) opted to partake in this optional program. Each state, in turn, has its own agency that administers its Medicaid program given federal requirements. Eligibility, therefore, is determined by both federal and state law. It involves various factors, such as age, disability, place of care, asset limits, income limits, etc. It impacts both the applicant and the applicant's spouse.

SEEING MEDICAID'S FUTURE

The Executive Summary of the Department of Health and Human Services' 2017 Actuarial Report on the Financial Outlook For Medicaid (DHHS Report) reported that:

> Medicaid expenditures are estimated to have increased 2.6 percent to $592.2 billion in 2017, with federal expenditures having grown an estimated 1.7 percent to $360.6 billion. The federal share of all Medicaid expenditures is estimated to have been 63 percent in 2017. States cover the remaining percentage. Their Medicaid expenditures, in turn, were estimated to have increased 4.2 percent to $221.6 billion.[48]

The DHHS Report made projections to year 2026 for the outlook of the Medicaid program. It projected "expenditures to increase at an average annual rate of 5.7% by year 2026. Yet, the U.S. Gross Domestic Product (GDP) is expected to grow by an average rate of only 4.1 percent."[49] In addition, according to the

DHHS Report, beginning in 2014, the expansion of Medicaid under the Affordable Care Act caused a "significant increase in expenditures and enrollment."[50] Table 2 of the Report, showing Historical and Projected Medicaid Enrollment and Expenditures, projects an increase of enrollment by year 2026 to 82.3 million people for a total cost of $1,005,700,000 (over one billion dollars) with the federal government accounting for $623,600,000 of the cost and states accounting for over $382,100,000 in costs. This compares to 2016 costs of $364,500,000 and $212,700,000, respectively.[51]

Focusing on just fee-for-service LTC (non-facility care), such expenditures are expected to increase by 3.2 percent on average through the year 2026.[52] The Americans with Disabilities Act of 1990, as interpreted by the U.S. Supreme Court in *Olmstead v. L.C.* (119 S. Ct. 2176 (1999)), mandates that states must provide community-based placement for the disabled when appropriate and consistent with consumer wishes.[53] Although the DHHS Report states that such home care may drastically reduce public expenditures, it also explains that although private pay for home care eases Medicaid funding, "many people who pay privately for nursing home care or community-based long-term care become impoverished due to the expense; as a result, these people eventually become eligible for Medicaid."[54] Consider how women live longer than men and the factors discussed in Chapters Four and Five. No wonder women are disproportionately impacted by poor planning.

Medicaid increasingly represents a large percentage of the federal budget. According to the President's fiscal year 2019 budget, by year 2027, Medicaid is projected to represent 9.2 percent of Federal expenditures. According to the National Association of State Budget Officers (NASBO), such expenses for all states in fiscal year 2016 represented 28.7 percent.

FORESEEING THE NATION'S ECONOMIC FUTURE

The report is bleak for the future of the unprepared. As we saw in Chapter Six, many people not only underinvest for retirement and other life stages, but also are woefully unprepared financially for their End-Stage security. Consider further other pressures on the federal budget. The Summary of the 2019 Annual Reports by the Social Security and Medicare Boards of Trustees on the Status of the Social Security and Medicare Programs reported that "Social Security and Medicare together accounted for 45 percent of federal program expenditures (excluding net interest on the debt) in fiscal year 2018."[55] In addition, "Both Social Security and Medicare will experience cost growth substantially in excess of GDP growth through the mid-2030s due to rapid population aging caused by the large baby-boom generation entering retirement and lower-birth-rate generations entering employment." In short, the trustees estimate that by year 2034, Social Security benefits will be reduced to only 79 percent of one's full eligible benefits, assuming no change in law. Further, although lower than the U.S. 2019 fiscal year budget deficit, the fiscal year 2020 budget (October 1, 2020 through September 30, 2021) created over a $1 trillion deficit. This budget was created *before* the government's financial efforts to combat the COVID-19 virus's devastating impact upon the U.S. people and economy.

Relying solely on Medicaid benefits for your End-Stage security may be the worst plan for your future. As the saying goes: The writing is on the wall.

PREPAREDNESS QUESTIONS

1. How financially sound do you expect the U.S. Medicaid system to be when you need it?

2. How confident are you about relying on Medicaid for your End-Stage security plan?

3. Revisit your expected Social Security benefits. If the government reduces your Social Security benefits, consider your investment projections. Adjust your budget if necessary.

CHAPTER TWELVE

SHELTERING ASSETS FROM PREDATORY ATTACK

"Wealth is the ability to fully experience life."

— Henry David Thoreau

What if you accomplish the challenge of this book and accumulate the wealth that you desire for your, and your family's, financial security? How then may you efficiently shelter it? No matter how much wealth you have, predators might take it, especially if you or your beneficiaries are vulnerable to their attacks. More vulnerable individuals are doctors, businesspeople, entrepreneurs, entertainers, or simply individuals, families, and family business owners, who have carefully built their wealth and want to ensure it is protected. Who might be these predators? You never know who might seek to take what you have; it may be an aggrieved litigant, federal or local governments through their taxing authorities, a divorcing spouse, a creditor, or a healthcare institution for expenses due to a prolonged illness. It might even be a family beneficiary through his or her spendthrift habits. Although many creative options exist to shelter assets and protect beneficiaries, this chapter explores some advanced estate planning methods to shelter wealth against attack. The type of trust created, the grantor's purpose for the trust, the type of assets that the trust may hold, the needed duration of the trust to accomplish the trust purpose, trust situs (state jurisdiction), estate and income taxes, and fraudulent transfer statutes all must be considered. Thus, these trusts are intricate and complex.

CONSIDERING TYPES OF TRUSTS

When it comes to using trusts to shelter assets, there are two general types of trusts to understand with one interesting exception. The first is self-settled trusts whereby you create a trust for your benefit and usually also appoint yourself as trustee. You thus would be the grantor, trustee, and beneficiary of the trust and would have full control over the management and disposition of trust assets. As mentioned previously, these trusts are generally revocable and their assets are included in your gross taxable estate for estate tax purposes. This type of trust provides no sheltering of assets from your creditors, even if a trustee other than yourself is given full discretion to distribute trust assets to other beneficiaries along with yourself. This concept is a long-recognized principle that comes from our British common law with the Statute of 3 Henry VII in 1487.

The other general type of trust is a non-self-settled trust (or third-party trust) in which the grantor creates the trust for the benefit of individuals or entities other than him- or herself. Some examples of this type of trust are testamentary trusts, some charitable trusts, dynasty trusts, and other specifically designed irrevocable trusts. A testamentary trust is one created in a decedent's will; thus, the maker is dead at the time it is created. The other inter-vivos (living) trusts that a grantor may create may take effect while he or she is alive or upon death and, if properly drafted, may shelter assets appropriately transferred to it. Another difference from self-settled trusts is that these trusts are their own taxable entity, with their own tax identification number. Conversely, the tax identification of your revocable trust (or an irrevocable grantor trust specifically drafted to include income to the grantor and not the trust, often called defective grantor trusts) is your Social Security number, and all matters of income and expense pass to you individually, to be reported on your own income tax return. The interesting exception is a domestic asset protection trust (DAPT or domestic APT), which is a self-settled trust that allows the grantor to be a beneficiary and still provides creditor protection.

All of these non-self-settled (and domestic asset protection) trusts are irrevocable and involve advanced tax and estate planning. Another key feature is a spendthrift clause. For this reason, some of these trusts are called spendthrift trusts. Basically, a spendthrift clause prohibits creditors of a beneficiary from attacking trust assets designated for that beneficiary. It also prohibits the beneficiary from assigning or pledging trust assets held for his or her benefit to another "third" party. Although asset sheltering involves a consideration of other trust clauses and the application of law, the spendthrift clause is like a trust gatekeeper: no assets may escape or be attacked, other than pursuant to the distribution, withdrawal, or administrative expense provisions of the trust. Robust and properly drafted spendthrift clauses are an essential feature for trusts designed to shelter assets and protect the trust's beneficiaries. Which type of trust you choose, however, first depends upon the assets you seek to shelter and for what purpose or purposes.

DETERMINING TRUST PURPOSE

1. Reducing Estate Taxes and Life Insurance

If the goal is to remove the death benefit and accumulated cash of life insurance from your gross taxable estate for estate tax purposes, transferring life insurance policies to an Irrevocable Life Insurance Trust (ILIT) is an attractive estate planning option. After the use of revocable trusts for a married couple, an estate planning attorney typically next looks at sheltering life insurance benefits to lower or avoid estate taxes. Although a life insurance policy does not pay its benefits until the death of the insured, the policy has a value, which when transferred to the ILIT, is considered a taxable gift. This value is called the interpolated terminal reserve value, and it generally consists of the cash value at the time of the transfer to the trust, plus a prorated value of the premium coverage remaining after the transfer. The best tax scenario is to create your ILIT when purchasing life insurance to avoid this gift tax issue. If the transfer of the policy, and any future premium payments for the policy, are within the annual exclusion amount for each beneficiary, the gift tax may be avoided, but only if the transfer is considered a present interest under the IRC. Otherwise, the gift is taxable, must be reported on a gift tax return, and reduces the applicable estate tax exemption when you, as the owner, die. This tax treatment is avoided by carefully drafting provisions in the ILIT that enable a beneficiary a short window of time to withdraw his or her proportionate share of the asset transferred, which includes future premium payments. This window of opportunity makes the gift a present interest—not a future benefit when the insured dies—and thus makes the annual exclusion of the IRC applicable. Optimally, if the proportionate premium amount for each trust beneficiary is below the annual exclusion, the premium "gifts" are also non-taxable. An ILIT may also be referred to as a Crummey Trust, based upon a claim by Clifford Crummey who challenged the IRS's denial of the annual exclusion application in the 1960s. The judge disagreed with the IRS, and today, notice to beneficiaries of their withdrawal right is commonly called a "Crummey" notice. The drawback is if a beneficiary actually withdraws his or her proportionate gift amount.

2. Making Charitable Gifts

If you have a charitable purpose, you may take advantage of deductibility of income for your estate with a gift to qualifying charities. If the gift is made when alive, you may qualify for a deduction from your taxable income. If the gift is made upon death, you are entitled to a deduction from your GTE. If you purely seek a charitable deduction from your GTE to avoid estate taxes (and benefit one or many charities), an outright distribution at death might be appropriate. Various types of charitable trusts may be designed depending upon your objectives and within the IRC. You might create an income stream to you or other beneficiaries for a term or for life, with the remainder trust assets passing to a charity or multiple, perhaps tiered, charitable beneficiaries.

Ideal assets to fund charitable trusts are highly appreciated assets. The reason is when you transfer assets to an irrevocable trust, it is a gift and the cost basis of the asset "carries over" to the trust. In other words, once transferred, the asset has the same cost basis in the trust as it did when the grantor owned it. When transferring assets to non-charitable irrevocable trusts, the cost basis is an issue when a distribution is made to a beneficiary since there will be a distribution of gain (appreciation) and an accompanying income tax. With charitable trusts, this is not the case. The charity receives the asset income tax free. The gain disappears for charitable beneficiaries. However, for charitable remainder trusts in which you receive an income stream, you still have an income tax on the income, similar to withdrawals from qualified retirement accounts.

3. Sheltering a Second Home—Qualified Personal Residence Trusts

Another sheltering option involves placing a home into a specially designed irrevocable trust, called a Qualified Personal Residence Trust (QPRT) since it possesses many particular qualifications by the IRC regulations. The trust benefits family members, generally successor generations, after you. The real property is transferred to the QPRT, so you gift the value of the home, but not the right to use it for a specified time period. This time frame is considered a retained interest in the property, called a "reserved" term, which has a value. This retained value, along with other variables at the time of the property's transfer to the QPRT, reduces the full property value gifted to your remainder beneficiaries and, in return, any applicable gift tax. Some of the specific benefits and qualifications for a QPRT are:

- It shifts wealth to the next generation to avoid estate taxes, assuming the grantor lives past the reserved term. The grantor must survive the reserved term to remove the full value of the property from his or her gross taxable estate. If the grantor dies prior to the expiration of the reserved term, the full property value reverts back to the grantor's taxable estate.
- The gift provides an immediate transfer of appreciation in value to the successor family (beneficiary) generations. The value of the property at the time of transfer is a factor, however. The term, applicable federal interest rate in the month of the transfer, and the grantor's age, all are variables in an equation that determines how much of the full property value is a taxable gift. The longer the term, the higher the interest rate, and the younger the grantor, the lower the taxable gift amount. The key is for the term to be short enough for a high likelihood that the grantor survives it but long enough to reduce the taxable gift amount.

- It transfers property used for personal use, which generally is difficult to exempt from estate taxes. Disadvantages are that during the reserved term, the trust is considered a grantor trust, making the income taxes on the property taxable to the grantor. If the grantor has a taxable estate, however, this may not be a disadvantage since it reduces further the grantor's estate to the benefit of the family "remainder" trust beneficiaries with no accompanying gift or estate tax.
- As long as the grantor lives past the reserved term, all appreciation (gain) passes to the remainder beneficiaries and escapes estate taxes in the grantor's estate. The negative is that upon sale of the residence, the remainder beneficiaries receive the tax burden. The remainder beneficiaries receive the same cost basis that the grantor possessed at the time of the property's transfer to the trust.
- Since the gift is for remainder beneficiaries in the future (after the reserved term), the annual exclusion does not apply. Therefore, some of the full value of the gift is taxable, which reduces the grantor's estate tax exemption upon death.
- No income or principal may distribute to the remainder beneficiaries until after the reserved term (or prior

death of the grantor).

- The trust may not hold cash greater than that needed for the upkeep and maintenance of the residence.
- A person may place only one residence in a QPRT, enabling each spouse to transfer a home to a QPRT.

If you have a second home that is expected to appreciate in value over your lifetime, adding a QPRT to your estate plan to own it not only provides tax benefits, but may allow for unity in management of a potentially contentious family asset. With multiple owners, especially over time, sharing the maintenance and use of a second home for many family members is problematic. After the expiration of the reserved term, the grantor may rent the property, paying fair rent to the QPRT, which transfers more wealth to the next generation, gift/estate tax free. If not, the property may transfer out to the remainder family members or optimally into their own revocable trusts. It also may be sold with the net proceeds going to the remainder beneficiaries.

Your primary home may not be the best asset to fund a QPRT. The reason is IRC §121, which allows $250,000 in tax-free gain for each spouse (up to $500,000 total) as long as the owner lived in the home for at least two of the prior five years when transferring the property. This Code section does not apply to non-primary homes, making them more ideal to use for QPRTs.

4. Providing for Family—Dynasty Trusts

If your planning goal is to provide a safety net for family members, especially multiple generations, consider a dynasty trust. Another purpose for using a dynasty trust may be to shelter assets away from your taxable estate. Of all the advanced trusts discussed in this chapter, the dynasty trust likely is the most customizable trust for the grantor's purposes. It is an ideal estate planning tool if you seek to:

- Encourage (family) values
- Transfer and build wealth for family
- Provide for educational costs
- Protect generations of family members
- Teach wealth management or at least postpone the management until the beneficiary is mature and able to do so
- Teach philanthropy
- Ensure the continuation of a family business and its mission

By gifting assets valued below the annual exclusion amount for each trust beneficiary, you may transfer a large amount of wealth to a dynasty trust without a gift tax (or concomitant estate tax) over a long duration of time. For instance, husband and wife clients had three children and seven grandchildren when they met their attorney. After discussing their estate planning objectives, as part of their overall plan, they decided to execute a dynasty trust, making their children and grandchildren the beneficiaries. Every year until the husband died twelve years later, they each gifted to the dynasty trust the applicable annual exclusion amount for that year, times the ten beneficiaries. Over the twelve-year gifting period, they sheltered over $2.6 million for the benefit of their family, escaping gift and estate taxes. This sheltering was in addition to the estate tax exemption amount that the husband's estate did not have to pay when he died. In fact, the plan worked as neither his nor her estate, upon her later death, had to pay any estate taxes.

The next key consideration is what attributes you wish to encourage or provide for your beneficiaries. If your goal is to build wealth or hold the outright distribution of your wealth until a beneficiary is mature and learned enough to manage it, you could postpone distributions, although the present interest concern discussed above must be handled. To make the annual exclusion applicable, the trust could be designed to distribute only income with a delay of principal distributions. The trust also may provide for the beneficiary's education, or also include health/medical needs. In this manner, you also assist younger beneficiaries, as well as their parents, with the burden of building enough wealth to educate their children or eliminate their incurring debt to receive the benefits of a better or advance education. Providing for grandchildren this way is especially helpful if your child chooses a career that may be personally rewarding but not financially lucrative. This incentive trust may also provide inducements of principal distributions when the beneficiary engages in certain favorable activities such as being admitted to college, marriage, birth of a child, etc., thus encouraging and enhancing family values. A concern, however, is enabling a beneficiary through poorly considered, but well intentioned, trust distribution provisions. In such a case, the trust could provide so much comfort that it causes a disincentive for a beneficiary to learn how to "hunt and fish" in life. In other words, the beneficiary may forgo the educational and vocational education and experience for healthy self-sufficiency.

A dynasty trust also provides an excellent opportunity to encourage a societal responsibility in others through encouraging philanthropy efforts. This goal can be accomplished in numerous ways, but one simple way is to empower the trustee to make a certain amount or percentage of charitable distributions each year to charities the beneficiaries choose (although not to a family foundation in which the grantor of the trust is a disqualified person). If done properly, the dynasty trust may be managed in conjunction with a private family foundation.

Lastly, a dynasty trust is a useful tool for the management of a family business. One concern with a family business is its continued success with successive generations. On average, only about 30 percent of family businesses survive to the second family generation, with only about 12 percent surviving to the third generation.[56] Another concern is family disharmony with certain individuals or families having control over the business. Instead, the trust may own the business with a carefully considered voting panel that makes business decisions with the objective of eliminating such disharmony.

One example is a client who was concerned his children might engage in negative behaviors. He formed a dynasty trust to hold and distribute his self-made millions not only to avoid estate taxes upon his death but to protect his children. He included trust provisions that instructed the trustee to provide for a beneficiary's health and education costs up to a certain age, but for the beneficiary to receive any additional income or principal of their respective trust share, they had to prove they were in school, working, and paid income taxes the previous year, or a combination of the two at given percentages. A low principal distribution percentage was established upon the client's death, which increased yearly according to the Cost of Living Index. This client did not want his children to engage in any lazy habits and live off of his hard-earned wealth.

If you are considering a dynasty trust, first carefully consider your intentions and objectives to educate your estate planning attorney so he or she may properly draft the trust to last for generations with robust provisions for success that enhance your family goals.

KNOWING TRUST DURATION, SITUS, AND INCOME TAXES

Two key features for non-self-settled trusts and DAPTs (domestic asset protection trusts) besides purpose are their duration and situs. The trust duration depends upon the state laws of the trust situs. Except for charitable trusts, duration depends upon a common law concept called the rule against perpetuity. The common law rule against perpetuity invalidates a transfer of an interest in property if it may fail to vest within twenty-one years after the lives in being when the interest was created. In other words, if for some reason the interest does not transfer to a beneficiary alive upon the creation of the irrevocable trust plus twenty-one years, that transfer is invalid from the start. This rule originated in England in the seventeenth century to encourage the alienation of property and because beyond this time period it was viewed as an excessive limitation on the use and ownership of property. The harshness of the common law rule has been altered statutorily by twenty-nine states, commonly allowing a maximum term of a set number of years, such as ninety years. However, in an effort to attract income tax revenue from trusts, an increasing number of states have eliminated this rule altogether. Presently, nineteen states allow a trust to exist for a much longer duration. For an individual seeking to shelter assets from creditors and protect beneficiaries, these states provide a plethora of jurisdictional choices from which to choose. This allows you to forum shop for the situs of such trusts.

Besides sheltering assets, avoiding or limiting income taxes is another major consideration for choosing a trust situs. However, one may not simply draft that a state's income taxes do not apply or that another state's income tax laws apply. Many states consider the residence of the trust grantor as the determining factor for income tax liability. In other states, the determining factor is where the beneficiaries or trustee resides, or where the trust is administered. For real property, its location may control for tax purposes. For this reason, estate planners seek to transfer the ownership of the real property to a limited liability company (LLC), which, in turn, is owned by a trust. Since these trusts are designed to continue for a long duration, often the trusts empower an independent trustee or a trust protector with the authority to change the trust situs.

LEARNING ABOUT DOMESTIC ASSET PROTECTION TRUSTS (DAPTS)

If your main estate planning purpose is to protect assets

from your own potential future creditors, then consider an asset protection trust. A domestic asset protection trust (DAPT) is an irrevocable, self-settled trust in which the grantor may be a beneficiary. Properly drafted, the trust shelters its assets from unknown future creditors (at the time assets are transferred to the trust). DAPTs generally do not shelter assets from:

- valid pre-transfer claims
- post-transfer claims brought within the statute of limitations time frame pursuant to the laws of the DAPT jurisdiction (often four years, although for some states it is less)
- family claims, such as alimony, child support, or other such settlement agreements
- tortious claims

Nineteen states presently legally allow a DAPT, with Connecticut joining the group in the year 2020. The present DAPT jurisdictions are Alaska, Connecticut, Delaware, Hawaii, Michigan, Mississippi, Missouri, Nevada, New Hampshire, Ohio, Oklahoma, Rhode Island, South Dakota, Tennessee, Utah, Virginia, West Virginia, and Wyoming. Each state has its own legal nuances for its DAPT creation. An additional advantage to asset protection may be limiting state income taxes, depending upon the situs of the trust. When considering the trust's purpose and the assets to fund the trust, many factors must be analyzed. They deal with matters of legal protection, taxation, business type, and distributions to the grantor and family beneficiaries. You, and your lawyer, must carefully consider all of these matters since the trust is irrevocable.

The laws of the chosen DAPT jurisdiction must be carefully followed. For instance, some DAPT jurisdictions may not allow a grantor to reserve the right to income from trust assets. Thus, it is critical that the laws of the DAPT jurisdiction you choose support the trust's purpose. In general, to withstand creditor attacks, a properly drafted DAPT must: 1) contain a robust spendthrift clause; 2) provide that the laws of the chosen DAPT jurisdiction govern the trust's validity, construction, and administration; and 3) have a substantial relationship to the DAPT jurisdiction, which generally involves choosing a qualified trustee such as an individual residing in that jurisdiction or a corporate trustee legally authorized to administer trusts in such jurisdiction. Only assets you intend to hold for a long term should be considered because withdrawals from the trust should be infrequent and well analyzed. Usually, the grantor may not be a trustee. The trust should also have other beneficiaries besides the grantor.

While the full faith and credit clause of the U.S. Constitution forces an out-of-state creditor litigant to honor the laws of your DAPT state, the U.S. Constitution also contains a supremacy clause, which provides that the federal government's laws trump state law. Therefore, although the DAPT may shield individual attacks, do not assume the trust's spendthrift clause will shield an attack in federal bankruptcy court. U.S. Bankruptcy Code 11 U.S.C §541(c)(2) is nuanced, and depending on the court's interpretation of the trust's spendthrift and distribution clauses, the court may conclude that a beneficiary (such as the grantor) possesses the right to demand money from the trust and rule that the beneficiary, such as the grantor, must access trust assets to satisfy his or her debt in bankruptcy.

Another concern is the drafting lawyer's ethical obligations and fraudulent transfer statutes. All states but California have ethical rules that prohibit lawyers from engaging, or assisting a client, in criminal or fraudulent conduct. Fraudulent transfer statutes generally state that the grantor may not transfer any asset with the intent to hinder, delay, or defraud a creditor, or without fair and adequate value. Therefore, do not be surprised if the drafting lawyer engages in a thorough investigation of you, your past, and especially circumstances that may reveal that a claim exists when transferring assets to the trust. Again, fraudulent transfer statutes and ethical rules vary by state and must be carefully evaluated.

A last general consideration is providing asset protection around an asset placed in trust. For instance, if you seek to place in the DAPT a business, rental real estate, or assets with higher risk associated with their use, such as boats, aircraft, motor homes, etc., consider further asset protection. One way is additional insurance coverage. Another is to have these assets be owned by a limited liability company (LLC), which in turn is an asset of the trust. Now all lawsuits dealing with the underlying asset are shielded by the protections afforded the LLC, with two exceptions. One exception is that a single member LLC may not provide asset protection because a court may deem this business form to be a pass-through entity to the sole owner. Another exception is that in order to have the asset sheltering benefit of an LLC, it must have a business purpose for holding and operating its assets.

With focused intentions, careful planning, and adroit drafting, trusts are flexible enough to provide a talented drafter the tools to create the appropriate canvas for you to shelter assets and simultaneously provide for other individuals and charities. Whether your intentions are to avoid taxes, protect beneficiaries, maintain privacy, provide charitable gifts, foster family values, or shelter wealth, trusts are a useful and valuable estate planning tool for you to consider.

A FINAL NOTE

ACHIEVING PEACE OF MIND

"In time all things come to pass."

— Hon. Judge John Reynolds
(Connecticut Superior Court)

The opening of this book introduced a perceived gap in preparedness of seniors for their End-Stage security and concluded that discussion with a bleak report of the future financial health of public assistance in the United States, given decreasing anticipated revenues and increasing demands for long-term care. Hence, this book's main purpose has been to provide you with the knowledge to prepare your own End-Stage security. Although a bit complex to grasp, understanding the time-value of money and the rate of return that you will need, given the duration you have to invest, will provide the power you need to effectively prepare yourself.

As illustrated in Chapter Six, few people adequately invest

for retirement; even fewer understand what their End-Stage issues and ensuing costs would look like. The intent was to illustrate a likely End-Stage outlook and provide you with the tools to prepare for it, hopefully well in advance, so you will not face the issues that Ellen in Chapter One, and so many people today, abruptly face.

Preparing yourself financially in order to build adequate wealth for your later years is not the only unknown. Understanding how to protect your assets, especially given changing challenges in your life, is equally important. For this reason, estate planning concepts were presented with suggestions for changes during different stages of your life, including, perhaps, the most important time—when the End-Stage event occurs. Also discussed were probabilities for needing long-term care, the duration of its need, and the ability to leverage its costs through insurance to achieve the goal of protecting your assets and creating peace of mind. A book like this would not be complete without introducing other aging issues, such as financial abuse and spotting declining faculties before explaining the Medicaid application process itself. Housing issues were presented to demystify other viable, and perhaps safer, living considerations outside the home. And, of course, the book presents a continual discussion of long-term care and Medicaid preparedness. For those individuals who accomplished the investment challenge and accumulated wealth, the book concludes with a chapter on numerous advanced estate planning ways to protect that wealth.

Ultimately, the objective was to provide a full picture of a potential future based upon unpreparedness so you may understand the issues involved and create the comfortable life you desire even after a debilitating End-Stage event. With this knowledge and understanding, no matter where you presently are on your life's course, you may clearly define your desired path, embrace your deservability of that desire, and take action to achieve it.

So what actions will you undertake now to create your End-Stage security? To get started, use Exhibit C to list ten things you have learned in this book that you will implement in the next ninety days. I encourage you to contact me and tell me what you liked, or disliked about the book, as well as to offer any ideas you would like me to expand or further discuss so I may improve readers' experience for the next edition. More importantly, please let me know about you, your challenges, your obstacles, and your adversities so I may better assist you with your journey. I would be glad to offer you a complimentary, no obligation, 30-60-minute audio, video, or in person (if geography permits) consultation to see how my legal services might help you or your loved one. My contact information is: vincent@preparingforyourelderyears.com. Please provide time zone and best times to schedule your complimentary consultation.

Good luck and be well! I wish you success, prosperity, and good health.

APPENDICES

Hopefully, by now I have made my case that you need to be prepared for your elder years. However, no argument would be complete without introducing all the evidence, so in the following pages, I offer for your consideration the exhibits to support my claims. After you have reviewed them, hopefully you will do everything you can to make sure you or your loved one are prepared for all stages of your life, especially ultimately for End-Stage issues.

EXHIBIT A

TEN COMMON MISTAKES IN MANAGING YOUR AFFAIRS

1. **Believing your will is an estate plan and that it will always work.** Matters such as probate rules, real estate laws, laws for income (including capital gains), gift and estate taxes, beneficiary designations, how title to an asset is held, and changes in family circumstances (including births and deaths), all impact how and to whom your assets pass. For some estates, holding assets jointly or having only a will is the worst "estate plan" if your goal is to save taxes and protect family members.

2. **Having erroneous expectations and failing to plan.** Many people think they will not die soon, can effectively manage their affairs despite the changing phases of their lives, and their will is all that will be needed to handle their estate when they die. In our early years, guardianship for our dependents and retirement savings seem paramount. In our later years, long-term care costs, medical and pharmaceutical costs, and not outliving our assets take precedence. Continuous, routine review of how your assets are titled and how they are distributed given your estate plan is the only way to maximize

your wishes and minimize costs and expenses associated with death. The key focuses of estate planning are to determine if assets are titled properly, to consider how you wish your assets to pass at death, to review all beneficiary assets like life insurance policies, to assess how to pay for long-term care at the end-stages of life, and to make sure your standard of living does not decrease over time or after the loss of a spouse. Asset protection and business succession planning may also be a focus.

3. **Failing to plan for incapacity.** A medical directive (advanced healthcare directive) is an essential part of one's estate plan. Incapacity could befall any of us at any time. For this reason, I advise my clients to have a child sign a medical directive when the child attains age eighteen. This simple document could avoid family strife and the costs and court interference of a conservatorship action. In it, you simply appoint who you want to make medical decisions for you when you are unable to do so yourself. To handle financial matters when incapacitated, one should sign a durable power of attorney and carefully review the powers granted to the appointed agent in the document. As our lives change, these powers may need to be changed. For instance, should the document include powers regarding a business? Should it include gifting powers, and if so, should there be a limit? Does it allow your agent to com-

municate to doctors, hospitals, and continuing care facilities in order to pay for such expenses? Have laws changed that require the documents to change?

4. **Not updating your life insurance needs.** In the life insurance industry, products are continually improving with more innovative options given the changing times. A policy obtained today may provide greater flexibility and more coverage at less cost than a similar policy issued even five years ago. Given this constant industry evolution, it is as important to periodically review your life insurance and your designated beneficiaries—including contingent beneficiaries—as it is to review your estate plan.

5. **Failing to plan for long-term care costs.** Long-term care involves assistance with activities of daily living—eating, medication, toileting, ambulatory issues, dressing, etc. Health insurance does not cover long-term care needs, nor does Medicare. There are three ways to pay for long-term care costs: 1) self-pay, 2) spend down assets and qualify for Medicaid, or 3) if you have long-term care insurance, it pays for such costs. Average monthly home long-term care costs range from \$4,000–\$6,500, depending upon the type of care needed. Average monthly nursing home care varies by state with average costs of \$12,000–14,000 a month. To qualify for Medicaid, the applicant must reduce his assets to below \$1,600 (\$2,000

in some states) and his or her spouse may not have assets in excess of a yearly adjustable amount (excluding the home that is solely in the spouse's name).

6. **Improperly titling your assets.** Buying or holding an asset jointly with a spouse may be the worst plan given a couple's wealth. Giving one's home to children may likewise prove problematic. No matter what our wealth is, how we hold assets impacts capital gains taxes, gift taxes (which impact estate taxes), separation of assets due to a divorce decree, bankruptcy claims, creditor claims, etc. A good estate planner does not simply draft documents for you. He or she reviews and analyzes whether your assets are protected from the above issues, along with other concerns such as Medicaid and family issues, and then integrates this asset protection into the best estate plan. As life changes, the estate plan and how we title our assets within that plan may also change.

7. **Failing to review the designations of qualified investments or not having a contingent beneficiary appointed.** Too many people only choose "spouse" as the beneficiary of their IRA, 401(k), 403(b), and other qualified funds. Always designate a successor. If you die without a beneficiary, the asset becomes part of your probate estate and is subject to credit claims, divestment, taxes, etc. In addition, choosing a successor beneficiary may force you to consider other matters

such as whether those successor beneficiaries are capable and responsible enough to inherit such assets outright in their names. An overwhelming majority of beneficiaries choose to cash in such assets, paying penalties and taxes, instead of using the benefits of holding the asset as a component of their own investment strategy, and deferring income taxes. Also, do not assume that a beneficiary's creditors may not attach such assets, even if these assets are protected against creditors in your state. The state laws where the beneficiary lives, or moves to, will control whether the inherited qualified funds are protected against creditors, bankruptcy, spousal claims, etc. Sometimes a trust for a beneficiary's benefit is a better plan in order to protect them and the asset. This, too, should be discussed with both your financial planner and estate planner.

8. **Having the wrong financial planner.** Especially after 2008, people tend to be more skeptical of financial planners. Finding a good financial planner whom you trust, who truly knows the investment business and has your best interest at heart, is essential. Ask for referrals from other knowledgeable professionals whom you trust and interview financial planners for their knowledge, investment philosophy, and trustworthiness. Know what you want in a financial planner. Is he too institutional or too independent? Does she manage money or choose investments with money managers? How wide is his

scope of investments? What are the hidden costs of the suggested investments and has she thoroughly and candidly explained them to you? Very few of us can adequately maximize our investments for all changing facets of our lives. A good financial planner will take the time to ascertain your investment risk tolerance, goals/objectives, and lifetime needs. Ask for a projection of income and net worth past your expected life expectancy given your present investment plan and the one the financial planner proposes. Be completely honest about the person you wish to be and how you wish to live. The right investment strategy, with a lot of time to implement it, makes all the difference. The right financial planner will get you there.

9. **Asking the wrong lawyer to advise and draft your estate plan.** Knowing how your assets will pass at death, how the laws and rules of probate affect the transfer of this wealth, as well as all tax facets associated with this transfer, requires a lawyer who focuses his or her practice on estate planning and probate matters. A lawyer who knows real estate, business law, and even family law (especially divorce decrees and prenuptial agreements) may also be necessary given the circumstances of one's estate. Choose a lawyer knowledgeable with these areas of the law, not just any lawyer—no matter how nice he or she may be!

10. **Believing the family will "work it out."** Family dynamics change with the passing of a patriarch or matriarch, especially if the person favored, or appeared to have favored, one child over others. Do not leave the many aspects of wealth transfer to chance. Take the time to discuss the transfer of your estate, no matter what its value may be, with a knowledgeable estate planning lawyer. Too often, a "leave it to the kids to work it out" estate plan erodes family harmony and only benefits the lawyers hired to litigate their disagreements, which quite often are rooted in unresolved family issues.

EXHIBIT B

CREATING AN ESTATE PLAN

Developing and periodically reviewing a sound estate plan is the first, and most essential, step in estate planning. It has been estimated that about 50 percent of adults do not even have a will. And how many of the other 50 percent regularly review or update their older estate documents? Protecting oneself and one's heirs is the principal objective of estate planning. Do you have the right plan to fully protect yourself throughout your and your loved ones' lives? Will you outlive your assets? Will your spouse and heirs? Sometimes a simple review of one's beneficiary designations makes all the difference. The key focuses of estate planning are determining if your assets are titled properly, considering how you wish your assets to pass at death, reviewing all beneficiary assets like life insurance policies, assessing how to pay for long-term care at the end-stages of life, and making sure your standard of living does not decrease over time or after the loss of a spouse.

For example, consider a widow who lived a very comfortable life with her husband, who had a child from a prior marriage. She believed she would inherit their expensive home, her husband's interests in income-producing commercial real estate properties, and all other investments that kept her and her husband comfortable when he was alive. Based upon assurances from her husband, she believed any estate taxes due upon his death would be covered by his life insurance policy. She discovered too late that her husband had not availed himself of proper estate planning. When he died, she learned the beneficiary of the life insurance policy was her husband's former wife, who was not willing to share any of the insurance proceeds to pay estate taxes assessed on her ex-husband's estate. The husband's simple will contained a tax clause, one that many generalist lawyers use in their will drafting, that made the "residual" estate (the probate estate) liable for all estate taxes due. Life insurance proceeds are not part of the probate estate. So the ex-wife received the life insurance proceeds estate tax-free, despite an estate tax being due on the ex-husband's estate. Estate taxes—due nine months after death—had to be paid from the portion of assets the wife inherited through her husband's will, thus depleting her ultimate inheritance. She also discovered that two of the commercial real estate properties could not be sold quickly to pay the estate taxes. One property had a long-term lease subject to an option to buy and the other had extensive environmental waste that she, as the new owner, was legally responsible to remediate. As the appointed executor, she was fully liable for the estate taxes due as well. The inheritance that was to continue her accustomed standard of living never materialized. To cover probate costs, legal fees, and the estate taxes, she sold the marital home and moved to a one-bedroom apartment. Her life drastically changed for the worse when her husband died! A simple estate review and appropriate plan would have avoided her unfortunate change in life. This is one example of why having the proper plan makes all the difference.

So, how does a good estate planner devise the correct plan for clients? First, he or she gathers information on all assets, determines how they are titled, and spends the time to fully understand the client's goals, objectives, and concerns. An estate planning intake questionnaire and an informal discussion with clients is the best way to accomplish these tasks.

Second, the estate planner must skillfully devise how best to achieve these objectives in the most cost- and tax-efficient way. The questionnaire should ask many questions, not just about assets and title, but also about matters such as citizenship, whether the client is a veteran of war, whether the clients' children are mature enough to manage inherited assets, concerns for divorce, lawsuits or bankruptcy of children, the public nature of the probate process, the private nature of trusts, dependents with special needs, retirement concerns, cost basis of assets owned, etc. All aspects dealing with asset ownership, management, transfer (during life and upon death), as well as health and financial needs/concerns should be discussed.

Third, an estate planning lawyer determines the total value of all assets to determine the "gross taxable estate" of the clients and whether a state and/or federal estate tax is due. This analysis is one factor that determines whether it is advisable to have trusts as part of the eventual estate plan (or a carefully constructed gifting strategy) and whether insurance proceeds of existing life insurance policies will cover the expected estate tax upon death.

Fourth, the lawyer discusses how best to transfer the assets owned to the intended recipients (beneficiaries). This may simply involve an outright transfer upon death, as with a will or a plan to hold assets for the benefit of someone who may or may not be the intended outright recipient. For instance, assets may be held in a trust for the benefit of a surviving spouse and then pass to other beneficiaries upon the surviving spouse's death. For couples with taxable estates, this is a typical plan. This plan also fits well for couples with children from prior relationships in order to provide for a surviving spouse without disinheriting children, as an outright transfer via a will would do. A trust may also hold assets for beneficiaries who do not demonstrate an ability to properly manage assets, such as younger children or individuals who may be exposed to creditor claims, lawsuits, divorce, or bankruptcy. The trustee of the trust will be instructed as to what conditions to distribute income and principal of the trust assets to, or for the benefit of, the beneficiary. A properly drafted trust ensures against the beneficiaries pledging trust assets and beneficiary creditors attaching trust assets.

For example, the trust may instruct the trustee to provide for a beneficiary's health, education, and living expenses and then allow the beneficiary to withdraw trust assets at a later age, or to make partial withdrawals at successive ages. For beneficiaries who may be exposed to lawsuits or may have a taxable estate themselves, one could keep assets in a properly drafted spendthrift trust for the beneficiary's benefit, thus preventing creditors from attaching trust assets and preventing such assets from being included in the beneficiary's taxable estate.

One could also create an Incentive Trust that encourages beneficiaries to act in certain ways, such as pursuing further education, in order to receive additional trust funds. The trust could instruct the trustee to distribute portions of trust assets upon the beneficiary's achieving additional levels of education or other benchmarks.

Fifth, the lawyer discusses potential long-term care needs and how clients will pay for such costs. Although with any illness or accident an adult may require long-term care, the best time in one's life to purchase long-term care insurance is in one's late fifties.

Costs for average skilled or intermediate care vary by state and region, but expect such cost to be about $12,000 to $15,000 a month ($144,000 to $180,000 a year, respectively). Without long-term care insurance, a prolonged illness/disease could decimate assets available for a surviving spouse and family members.

If one has a closely held business or even rental real estate property, it also is essential to review how the business is titled, income tax aspects, asset protection matters, and business succession plans such as buy-sell agreements.

Estate planning is not a one-time creation of documents, but the careful, continual review of the overall composition of a client's assets and how they distribute according to the client's wishes. Through proper estate planning advice and implementation, one may carefully navigate the many tax, family, business, probate, disability, asset protection, and litigation issues that afflict wealth and family harmony. Ignoring these issues could have drastic consequences. One's most important ally is an experienced estate planning lawyer who can explain these many complicated issues in a simple, understandable, and professional manner. This lawyer also should be able to coordinate his or her efforts with other professionals such as financial planners, accountants, and insurance agents.

EXHIBIT C

CREATING AN ACTION LIST

1. ____

2. ____

3. ____

4. ____

5. ____

6. ____

7. ____

8. ____

9. ____

10. ____

EXHIBIT D

SAMPLE INTAKE QUESTIONS AN ESTATE PLANNING ATTORNEY MIGHT ASK

1. Do you wish to discuss charitable gifting?

2. Do you own a business with others?

3. Does the business have a written plan to pass on an owner's interest upon his or her death or retirement?

4. Do any of your dependents have any special needs?

5. Do you have any highly appreciated assets that may be subject to a capital gains tax?

6. Do you have a highly appreciated vacation or second home?

7. Do you have any other highly appreciated assets?

8. Have you or your spouse/partner been married before?

9. If yes, do you or your spouse/partner have any children from this previous relationship?

10. Do you or your spouse have children who have died leaving children?

11. Does anyone to whom you may be leaving part of your estate require any help or protection in managing money or other property?

12. Do you and your spouse have a pre-nuptial or post-nuptial agreement?

13. Are you a veteran of war who served during wartime for at least ninety days?

14. Do you have long-term care insurance?

15. Have you adopted a child or given a child up for adoption?

16. Have you lived in a community property state (Arizona, California, Idaho, Louisiana, Nevada, New Mexico, Texas, Washington, or Wisconsin)?

17. Do you have a will?

18. Do you have a revocable living trust?

19. Do you have an insurance trust?

20. Do you have a living will?

21. Do you have a charitable remainder trust?

22. Do you have a conservator appointed?

23. Do you have any other kind of trust?

24. Do you have a durable power of attorney?

25. Do you have a healthcare agent appointed?

26. Do you own any firearms—rifles, shotguns, pistols, revolvers, state regulated/banned firearms and equipment, or firearms and accessories covered under the National Firearms Act of 1934? (If so, we should discuss the transfer of these firearms. This issue may impact choice of executor.)

EXHIBIT E

ESTATE PLANNING ASSET INTAKE

ASSET SUMMARY:

Asset	Estimated Value & Title
Real Property	
Bank Accounts	
Bonds	
Stock	
Qualified Retirement Plan Assets	
Business Interests	
Sole Proprietorship	
Tangible Personal Property	
Life Insurance Policies	
Other Assets	
Estimated Total:	

EXHIBIT F

HOW DO YOU WISH YOUR ESTATE TO PASS?

Will (with Testamentary Trust children (grandchildren) only) OR Revocable Trusts

USING A WILL

State the name and address of the person you wish to serve as Executor of your will. Generally, your spouse would be your Executor, unless you designate otherwise.

» *An <u>EXECUTOR</u> is the person you appoint to carry out the directions and requests in your will and to dispose of your property according to the provisions in your will. A successor Executor should be appointed in the event your spouse predeceases you or you both die together.*

Please provide the following:

Executor Name: ______________________________

Address: ______________________________

Relationship: ______________________________

Successor Executor: ______________________________

Address: ______________________________

____

Relationship: ______________________________

If you do *not* wish to use a revocable trust (see below), the following are examples of how one may transfer probate assets.

1. Partners tend to provide that upon their death, their property passes:
   b. To surviving spouse or partner.
   c. If one's spouse or partner dies before him or her, the estate property will be divided in equal shares among all their living children.
   d. If a spouse/partner and a child have predeceased you, that child's share of the estate is distributed to his/her children (the grandchildren) in equal shares (*per stirpes*).

2. Unmarried persons with children provide that upon their death, their property passes:

    a. In equal shares to all the living children.

    b. If one or more children predecease you, that child's share of the estate is distributed to his or her children (the grandchildren) in equal shares (*per stirpes*).

USING A REVOCABLE LIVING TRUST

» *A REVOCABLE LIVING* TRUST *is often called a will substitute because it accomplishes the same objectives of a will (plus more!). A revocable trust is an attractive estate-planning tool because assets held in the trust avoid probate court and its time delays, costs, and public exposure. It retains title to real property, making probating the real property unnecessary. This fact is especially beneficial if you own property in two or more states to avoid an additional ancillary probate administration in the state where the property is located. If one has children from a prior relationship, a trust is an excellent means to provide for a non-parental spouse/partner and still provide for the children. But perhaps the greatest benefit of such trusts for spouses is it allows a couple to possess twice the state (and federal) exemption amounts without incurring estate taxes.*

Advantages:

1. It distributes property after your death.
2. It creates one receptacle for all your property.
3. It takes care of you—you are the trustee, and in case of disability, your appointed successor trustee manages the trust assets.
4. It is private—it does not go to probate court, which is a public process.
5. It is easy to create and maintain.
6. You can easily change or terminate it.
7. There are no adverse lifetime income tax consequences.
8. It does not disinherit children born of a previous relationship as a will might do.
9. It provides continuity in your affairs.
10. You can specifically plan for the estate tax. You can use both spouses' applicable state exemption amounts instead of losing the exemption when the first spouse dies as with the use of wills.
11. It is good in every state.
12. It is more difficult to attack, as opposed to a will.

Disadvantages:

1. You may not be comfortable holding your assets in trust.
2. You cannot put qualified funds—401ks or IRAs—into the trust during your life but you may for your beneficiaries.

3. Slightly more upfront cost.
4. In general, it may not be necessary, depending upon the value of one's estate, how those assets are held, and what one's estate planning objectives are.

Please provide the following:

Trustee's Name: ______________________________

Trustee's Address: ______________________________

____

Relationship *(if any)*: ______________________________

Trustee's Name *(successor)*: ______________________________

Trustee's Address: ______________________________

____

Relationship *(if any)*: ______________________________

Per Stirpes means if your first named beneficiary predeceases you, you wish that deceased person's children to inherit his or her parent's inheritance.

Per Capita means you wish the predeceased beneficiary's portion to go to your other heirs and not to the deceased beneficiary's children.

If using a Trust, at what age(s) do you wish your children/grandchildren to receive their inheritance—either outright (free from the trust) or having the right to request a certain percentage of trust funds?

Age(s):

Absolute right to receive, or *right to withdraw* funds?

____

____

Other ways to transfer trust assets to consider:

- Income and principal for health, education, and support to a certain age (twenty-three for example). Then the trustee has discretion to distribute principal under certain defined conditions such as for health and education until a final age (thirty or thirty-five for example).

- Withdrawal rights at certain ages and amounts such as 25 percent of a beneficiary's share value at age 30, 33.33 percent of the share value existing at age 35, 50 percent of the share value existing at age 40, and the remaining share amount at age 45.
- Complete discretion with the trustee to distribute income and principal for child's health, education, support, etc. May also have withdrawal rights or a final age for outright distributions.
- Trustee discretion to make distributions or loans of principal to adult children in special circumstances; e.g. to purchase a new home, a new business venture, etc.

1. Who should personal property (jewelry, automobiles, etc.) and household goods pass to?

____

____

____

2. Remaining property?

____

____

____

3. Are there are any specific items or amounts that you wish to give to individuals or to charity?

____

____

____

4. Catastrophe Clause: What if all of your direct (lineal) heirs die before (or simultaneously with) you? Who then do you wish your estate assets to go to?

____

____

____

MEDICAL DIRECTIVES

Do you wish to consider a LIVING WILL?

» *A LIVING WILL is a means to communicate to a treating doctor and family members your wish not to be kept alive by artificial means or "heroic" efforts in case a situation should arise in which there is not a reasonable expectation of your recovery from unconsciousness. Besides giving healthcare instructions, you may also appoint a healthcare representative, appoint an attorney-in-fact for you, and designate someone as conservator of your person if you should become incapacitated.*

Other key appointments and designations:

- **HEALTHCARE REPRESENTATIVE** *(the person who makes healthcare decisions when you are unable to do so)*:

  Primary *(Spouse/Partner)* Name:________________________

  Address: ________________________

  ____

  Relationship *(if any)*:________________________

  Successor Name: ________________________

  Address: ________________________

  ____

  Relationship *(if any)*:________________________

- Any or all **ANATOMICAL GIFTS** (If you wish to donate any organ(s) or your whole body)?

Yes For any purpose, even for medical or educational purposes.

Yes For transplantation purposes only. Exceptions: _______

____

No

- **CONSERVATOR OF YOUR PERSON** *(The person who assists you with your physical needs when you are unable to fully care for yourself; a "parent to an adult")*:

Primary *(Spouse/Partner)* Name: ____________________

Address: ____________________

____

Relationship *(if any)*: ____________________

Successor Name: ____________________

Address: ____________________

____

Relationship *(if any)*: ____________________

- **CONSERVATOR OF YOUR ESTATE** *(The person who assists you with your financial needs when you are unable to fully manage your finances)*:

Primary*(Spouse/Partner)*Name:_______________________

Address: _______________________

____

Relationship*(if any)*:_______________________

Successor Name: _______________________

Address: _______________________

____

Relationship*(if any)*:_______________________

FINANCIAL POWER

Do you wish to consider a **DURABLE POWER OF ATTORNEY?**

» *A DURABLE POWER OF ATTORNEY is also desirable as an estate-planning tool. A Durable Power of Attorney is a legal document in which one person (the principal) authorizes another person (the representative or agent) to act in place of the principal. This device is helpful in case you are unable (either because of health problems, being on vacation, temporary incapacity, etc.) to manage your daily affairs such as to hold and manage real and personal property, receive/deposit or write checks, pay bills, etc. or to fund your living trust if you are incapacitated.*

If you wish to make a Durable Power of Attorney, please state two individuals to whom you wish to give authorization to manage your personal affairs in case you are unable to do so:

1. ____

   ____

2. ____

   ____

BIBLIOGRAPHY

Bova, Alexandria Bova. "Here's Exactly How Much You Need to Retire in Your State." January 9, 2020. https://www.gobankingrates.com/retirement/planning/how-much-need-survive-retirement-state/

Guinan, Sylvia. *The Richness of Divorce: 7 Steps to Unwind Your Marriage with Love and Grace.* Saybrook, CT: Flower of Life Press, 2020.

Social Security Administration Website: https://www.ssa.gov/myaccount

Stanley, Thomas J. and William D. Danko. *The Millionaire Next Door.* Lanham, MD: Taylor Trade Publishing, 1996.

The MetLife Study of Elder Financial Abuse: Crimes of Occasion, Desperation and Predation Against America's Elders. https://vawnet.org/material/metlife-study-elder-financial-abuse-crimes-occasion-desperation-and-predation-against

Endnotes

1 Stanley, T. and Danko, W. Taylor Trade Publishing, 1996.

2 These definitions are designed to explain terms in a user-friendly fashion so that terms and concepts are understandable throughout this book. For this reason, they are somewhat general in nature. More exhaustive definitions certainly may be obtained.

3 U.S. Code §61.

4 Lenders, such as banks, give us money; we give them a Promissory Note ("Note"), which is a written promise to pay them back, and security on that Note, which is the Mortgage we give them, which the lender uses as a lien on our home (or other real property) as security if we breach (don't pay) the Note payments.

5 The Patient Protection and Affordable Care Act (2010).

6 This list is according to the Health Insurance Portability and Accountability Act of 1996 (Pub.L. 104-191, 110 Stat. 1936).

7 The 2019 Setting Every Community Up for Retirement Enhancement (SECURE) Act changed this age from 70½ to 72.

8 Technically, the process is called a Deceased Spouse's Unused (Estate Tax) Exemption or DSUE. Portability was made legal in 2010 through the Tax Relief Unemployment Insurance Reauthorization and Job Creation Act of 2010 ("TRUIRJCA").

9 Although the trend is for states to terminate or slowly increase exemption amounts, some states impose separate estate or inheritance taxes. Presently, eighteen states and the District of Columbia impose such taxes. The states are: Connecticut, Delaware, Hawaii, Illinois, Iowa, Kentucky, Maine, Maryland (the only state that levies both an inheritance and estate tax), Massachusetts, Minnesota, Nebraska, New Jersey, New York, Oregon,

Pennsylvania, Rhode Island, Vermont, and Washington.

10 With the availability of portability federally, this doubling of the estate tax exemption is more a concern in states that have their own estate tax exemption where the portability feature is not available.

11 Some states, such as New York, have statutes that allow a grantor to amend an irrevocable trust.

12 Many types of irrevocable trusts may be discussed with estate planning lawyers knowledgeable in such areas. Some are discussed in the last chapter of the book.

13 Employee Retirement Income Security Act (ERISA).

14 See definition of LTC in Chapter Two.

15 altcp.org

16 United Nations - World Populations; 9ahref='https://www.macrotrends.net/countries/USA/united states/life-expectancy'>U.S.LifeExpectancy

17 Genworth 2018 Beyond Dollars Study, www.genworth.com

18 Home Instead Senior Care. "Crises in Caregiving: Workers Who Care for Aging Parents Face Personal and Professional Obstacles." Network Survey, 2019.

19 2019 U.S. Department of Health and Human Services (longtermcare.acl.gov)

20 Ellen Stark. AARP Bulletin. March 2018.

21 Genworth 2019 Cost of Care Survey by State, www.genworth.com

22 www.genworth.com, under the "Long-Term Care Insurance"

23 Genworth 2019 Cost of Care Survey, www.genworth.com

24 Matt Morton, FSA, MAAA, Senior Consulting Actuary for Long Term Care Group, Inc.

25 By Arielle O'Shea, Nerdwallet, as reported at: www.msn.com/en-us/money/theaverage401kbalance

26 Center for Nutrition Policy and Promotion www.cnpp.usda.gov; https://fns-prod.azureedge.net/sites/default/files/crc2015_March2017_0.pdf

27 https://ifstudies.org/blog/what-is-the-divorce-rate-anyway-around-42-percent-one-scholar-believes/

28 Personal interview with Sylvia Guinan. May 13, 2020.

29 Published January 9, 2020 by gobankingrates: https://www.gobankingrates.com/retirement/planning/how-much-need-survive-retirement-state/

30 https://www.metlife.com/assets/cao/mmi/publications/studies/zorr/mmi-elder-financial-abuse.pdf.

31 Ibid. p. 23

32 www.aarp.org

33 Enacted as part of the Patient Protection and Affordable Care Act, Pub. L. 111-148 (2010)

34 www.cdc.gov/violenceprevention/elderabuse/definitions.html

35 www.consumerfinance.gov.

36 http://ncea.aoa.gov/faq/index.aspx

37 42 U.S.C. §3001 et seq. (2006)

38 https://www.ncoa.org/public-polic)¡-action/lder justice/ elder-abuse-facts/.

39 DeLiema, Marguerite. *Elder Fraud and Financial Exploitation: Application of Routine Activity Theory*. Stanford Center on Longevity, Stanford University, California. Received August 18, 2016; Editorial Decision Date November 30, 2016. (Address correspondence to Marguerite DeLiema, PhD, Stanford Center on Longevity, Stanford University, Littlefield Center, 365 Lasuen Mall, 3rd Floor, Stanford, CA 94305-6053. E-mail: deliema@stanford.edu

40 Buckner, J. K., Duke, J. R. Jr., Good, J. T. Jr., et al. "Venous thromboembolism." In *Pulmonary Disorders of the Elderly*. Eds. T. L. Petty and J. S. Seebass JS. Philadelphia, PA: American College of Physicians, 2007.

41 CCRCs are also called Life-Care Communities. They are traditionally called nursing homes.

42 For further information, consult the Center for Medicare and Medicaid Services (CMS), which uses a five-star system to rate facilities, at Medicare.gov.

43 Armen Abrahamian, CLTC, CSA, a nationally recognized LTC planner, Long Term Care Insurance, LLC, 36 State Street, North Haven, CT 06473; www.ltcstrategies.com

44 Personal Interview with Armen Abrahamian. July 23, 2020.

45 Stillman & Associates LLC, 23 Boston Street, Guilford, CT 06437; mstillman@stillmanlegal.net. Matthew earned an LL.M. degree, and is licensed in Connecticut, New York, and Massachusetts.

46 Paul Spitalnic, ASA, MAAA, Statement from the Chief Actuary, Center for Medicare & Medicaid Services; 2017 Actuarial Report of the Financial Outlook For Medicaid, CMS (Centers for Medicare & Medicaid Services); Department of Health & Human Services.

47 Section 1902(a)(10)(A)(i)(VIII) of the Social Security Act [42 U.S.C. §1396a.

48 2017 Actuarial Report of the Financial Outlook for Medicaid, CMS (Centers for Medicare & Medicaid Services); Department of Health & Human Services. p. iv.

49 Ibid. p. v.

50 Ibid. p. 10.

51 Ibid. p. 12.

52 Ibid. p. 15.

53 Ibid. p. 16.

54 Ibid. p. 26.

55 U.S. Economy and News: Current U.S. Federal Budget Deficit by Kimberly Amadeo (Updated March 3, 2020); https://www.ssa.gov/oact/trsum/

56 Family Business Alliance. Retrieved June 2014: http://www.fbagr.org/index.php?option=com_content&view=article&id=117&Itemid=75.

ABOUT THE AUTHOR

VINCENT LIBERTI is an author, professional keynote speaker, law professor, and estate and elder law attorney whose practice focuses on sophisticated estate planning, elder law, business succession planning, probate administration and fiduciary representation, and real estate transactions, including IRC §1031 tax-deferred exchanges. He represents individuals (including lawyers for trust analysis), couples, fiduciaries, and family business owners.

Vincent earned a Bachelor of Science (B.S.) in Industrial Economics from Union College, a Juris Doctor (J.D.) in Law, and a Master of Laws (LL.M.) in Estate Planning and Elder Law from Western New England University School of Law. Vincent presently is licensed to practice law in the jurisdictions of New York, Connecticut, and Massachusetts as well as the Federal District Court for the District of Connecticut. He employs a down-to-earth approach with his legal representation that extends almost thirty years. Throughout his career, Vincent has been interviewed for television, radio, and in print on matters dealing with estate planning and same-sex marriage, pet trusts, reverse mortgages and the elderly, and various other creative estate planning issues.

An Adjunct Professor of Law at Western New England University School of Law's LL.M. degree program, Vincent teaches lawyers across the country in the post J.D. degree program on Estate Planning and Elder Law. He is married with an adult daughter and resides in Connecticut.

ABOUT THE LEGAL SERVICES OF VINCENT LIBERTI, J.D., LL.M.

Are you concerned about the high costs of senior care? Are you concerned about the long-term care costs of thousands of dollars a month for home care or over ten thousand dollars a month for facility care? Are you headed for a Medicaid spend-down plan for your long-term care? Do you understand and are you prepared for Medicaid? Have you executed the right estate plan for yourself, your partner, and family? If you are a high-net worth individual, have you adequately protected your wealth? Is your family also protected? If you own a family business, do you have a succession plan, and is it current?

If you are overwhelmed, exhausted, tired, do not know where to turn, or believe you need to enhance your estate to protect yourself from predators, then reach out to Vincent Liberti because he knows how you feel. He has almost thirty years' experience in helping people just like you to protect their estates, minimize taxes, shelter assets from predators, create iron clad trusts, provide long-term care advice, and devise estate plans that give the peace of mind you deserve.

If this process causes you to feel overwhelmed, avail yourself of the services of Vincent Liberti, a competent and experienced estate, elder, and business planning lawyer. He will be honored and thrilled to provide you with a 30-60-minute complimentary initial audio/video meeting to discuss your legal concerns. He may be reached at vincent@preparingforyourelderyears.com. Due to spam filters, in addition to an email, also text or call Vincent directly at (203) 971-9422.

BOOK VINCENT LIBERTI TO SPEAK AT YOUR NEXT EVENT

When it comes to choosing a professional speaker for your next event, you will find no one more respected or successful—no one who will leave your audience or colleagues with a more renewed passion for protecting their lives—than Vincent Liberti, one of the most gifted speakers of our generation. Since 1993, Vincent Liberti has delivered an abundance of inspirational presentations.

Whether your audience is 10 or 10,000, Vincent Liberti can deliver a customized message of inspiration for your meeting or conference. Vincent understands that your audience does not wish to be "taught" anything, but rather, it is interested in hearing stories of inspiration, achievement, and real-life people who created their own success.

As a result, Vincent Liberti's speaking philosophy is to humor, entertain, and inspire your audience with passion and stories proven to help people achieve extraordinary results. If you are looking for a memorable speaker who will leave your audience wanting more, book Vincent Liberti today!

To see a highlight video of Vincent Liberti and determine whether he is available for your next meeting, visit his site at the address below. Then telephone or email him to schedule a complimentary pre-speech phone interview.

www.PreparingforYourElderYears.com

vincent@preparingforyourelderyears.com

(203) 971-9422